SLAYING NAPLES

Curated by Leigh M. Clark

Aurora Corialis Publishing

Pittsburgh, PA

Printed in the United States of America
Edited by: Renee Picard, Aurora Corialis Publishing
Cover Design: Leigh M. Clark
Paperback ISBN: 978-1-958481-60-8
Ebook ISBN: 978-1-958481-61-5

OTHER COLLECTIVES BY LEIGH M. CLARK

Slaying Southwest Florida

Slaying Tampa Bay

Slaying Atlanta

Slaying Nashville

Slaying Sarasota

Slaying Chicago

Slaying Boston

Slaying Vegas

Slaying Orlando

Slaying New York

The Dream is in Your Hands

The Dream is in Your Hands: She Can Do It

Living Kindly: Bold Conversations About the Power of
Kindness

Table of Contents

Introduction
Leigh M. Clark

I was twenty-one the first time I came to Naples. Back then, my life was split between two worlds. By night, I was working long shifts at Pub 222 in St. Charles, Ill.—a place that became more than a job to me. Over the course of more than ten years, that pub was a second home. It was where I learned resilience, where I built friendships, and where I saw what community really looked like in its raw, unpolished form.

But when the late-night shifts ended, I didn't just collapse into bed like most people my age. I had another passion pulling me forward. By day, I was moonlighting at Clinique, learning the delicate balance of artistry and science. I learned how to match the undertones of a foundation to skin that told its own complicated story, how to paint on confidence with a steady hand, how to listen to a woman's insecurities and send her away standing a little taller.

Everyone at Pub 222 knew about my side hustle. I was the girl who could transform you before a date, touch up your lipstick before a night out, or give you the kind of beauty advice that made you feel like you'd just had a secret whispered in your ear. So when the pub decided to create a promotional calendar featuring all of the Pub Girls, it only made sense that I'd be the one behind the brush.

We did the big shoot back in Illinois—snow on the ground, bitter winds blowing outside, our breath rising in clouds between set-ups. But the glamorous part came after. My best friend Amy and I were invited to fly down to Naples, Fla., to meet with the bar owner and his wife. Our task was to sit in their sunlit home and sift through hundreds of photographs to decide which twelve would become the calendar.

On paper, it was just another project. But stepping off that plane in Naples, I had no idea I was walking into a love affair with a place that would one day become home.

First Impressions

The difference hit me immediately. In Illinois, winter is sharp and gray. The cold settles into your bones, and the sky hangs heavy like a lid. Naples was something else entirely. The air wrapped around me like silk—warm, humid, perfumed with plumeria and hibiscus. It smelled alive.

Driving through Naples for the first time, I felt like I had stumbled onto a movie set. Fifth Avenue glimmered with galleries and restaurants, the kind of scene where you could imagine a director calling "action" at any moment. Couples strolled hand-in-hand, families lingered over dinner on patios, and the palms swayed overhead like they'd been choreographed.

Even the colors felt exaggerated compared to the Midwest. Bougainvillea spilled in impossible shades of magenta across stucco walls. Hibiscus bloomed in fiery reds and oranges. Down by Marco Island, the water shimmered in tones I'd only ever seen in postcards. Everywhere, people seemed lighter—tanned, smiling, moving at a pace that suggested they'd figured out a secret the rest of us hadn't.

Coming from a world of icy parking lots and slush-stained boots, I was mesmerized. Naples was unapologetically beautiful, like it had nothing to prove. At twenty-one, I didn't know what to do with that kind of beauty, other than stand in awe. But even then, I felt the whisper of something bigger: this is what life could be.

The Road Back

It would be years before I returned. Life swept me up, as it does when you're chasing careers and paying bills and making choices that feel urgent but not always permanent. But in 2010, Naples came back into my life in a way that stuck.

By then, I was working for Groupon. My role was to uncover the best local deals, which meant exploring communities, talking to business owners, and finding the hidden gems that gave each city its flavor. When I moved to Southwest Florida, it became my job—and, honestly, my joy—to discover everything Naples had to offer.

I drove down Airport-Pulling Road, onto Goodlette-Frank, around Gulf Shore Boulevard, through neighborhoods that each told their own story. Some afternoons I wandered through Tin City, ducking into quirky shops that smelled like salt and sunshine, running my hands over trinkets while boats bobbed just outside the windows. When my parents visited, I brought them there too, proud to show off the charm, the history, the way this city seemed to balance polish and play so effortlessly.

What struck me most was the duality. Naples was luxury layered over simplicity. On one hand, it was estates with manicured lawns, high-end boutiques, golf courses so perfect they looked airbrushed. On the other, it was quiet canals where pelicans perched, family-owned restaurants tucked away from the main drag, neighbors waving as they biked past at sunset. Naples was glamorous and grounded at the same time.

Fifteen years later, I still love that duality. Naples is the only place in the world with two Ritz-Carltons, and that fact alone tells you a lot about the reputation it carries. But it's also a place where locals pack Publix subs and sit barefoot in the sand, watching the sun slip into the Gulf with reverence, like it's a show they've seen a thousand times and never grown tired of.

Planting New Roots

For me, Naples didn't just become home; it became the stage where my own story shifted. In 2023, I launched the very first book in what would become the Slay the USA series. That book—*Slaying Southwest Florida*—was born in Fort Myers, just a short drive up the coast. At the time, I had no idea it would grow into a national movement.

But it made sense to begin here. There's something about Southwest Florida that embodies resilience, creativity, and reinvention. This is a community of people who come from everywhere—Midwestern transplants, Northeastern snowbirds, native Floridians whose families go back generations—and they all weave themselves together into something vibrant. Naples, especially, has a way of elevating people, of making them dream a little bigger.

When the series began to expand into other cities, I always knew I'd come back to Naples. Because this city isn't just palm trees and pristine beaches. Naples is alive because of the women who call it home.

The Women of Naples

Everywhere I look here, I see women who inspire me. Women who have built businesses from scratch, turning passions into empires. Women who balance boardrooms and ballet recitals, who pour themselves into philanthropy, who lead with both grit and grace.

Some of these women are lifelong Floridians with roots stretching deep into the soil. Others are transplants who came here on vacation, fell in love with the Gulf, and decided to stay forever. Together, they create the heartbeat of Naples.

This city is known for luxury, and rightly so. But its real wealth lies in the people who shape it, challenge it, and give it its pulse. The women featured in this book are part of that fabric. They are visionaries, go-getters, leaders, artists, healers, creators. They are women who prove that Naples isn't just a beautiful backdrop—it's a living, breathing community where people leave their mark.

Coming Full Circle

When I think back to that twenty-one-year-old girl stepping off a plane with her best friend Amy, makeup brushes still tucked in her bag from a Clinique shift, I smile. She couldn't have known what Naples would one day mean to her. At the time, it was just a side trip, a work assignment, a glamorous detour from the Illinois winter.

But life has a way of circling back, of planting seeds you don't recognize until years later. Naples has been that for me—a place that started as a whisper and grew into a defining part of my life.

It's where I learned to slow down, to take in beauty without apology, to dream on a bigger canvas.

Now, as I introduce *Slaying Naples*, I feel both gratitude and awe. Gratitude for the journey that brought me here, and awe for the women who fill these pages with their stories. This isn't just another book in the Slay the USA series. This one feels personal.

Because Naples isn't just a city I fell in love with. It's home.

Behind the Mic, Beyond the Brand
Nicole Black & Kerri Kobakof

The Babes Who Built It
Welcome to Babes + Business

If you've ever felt like you were meant for *more*–more than a 9 to 5, more than the shoulds, more than playing small just to fit in–then babe, you're in the right place.

Babes + Business was never just about building businesses. It was about building *bold* women. It was about amplifying stories, unlocking purpose, and creating a place where women could finally take up space—in the boardroom, on the stage, and in their own damn lives. This is a movement built for the doers, the dreamers, the ones who are done pretending they're not powerful.

This is where your evolution begins.

It started like all great ideas do: messy, magical, and a little rebellious.

Meet the Hosts Behind the Mic
NICOLE BLACK – "The Hype Lady"

Nicole Black, aka *The Hype Lady*, had already been lighting up rooms for years. Known for her infectious energy, magnetic storytelling, and unapologetic truth bombs, she was the woman you called when you needed to remember who the hell you were. A mama, a mindset coach, and a multi-business maven with a decade of real estate and brand strategy under her belt, Nicole had one mission: to help women break cycles, get loud, and *build legacies*, not just businesses. She doesn't just hype you up; she helps you step into the next-level version of yourself through visibility, strategy, and energy.

Nicole's personal brand is rooted in confidence creation. She helps women believe in the magic of their message and the power of showing up consistently. Whether she's speaking on stage, leading an event, or helping a founder find her brand voice, Nicole brings clarity, charisma, and contagious belief.

But every visionary needs a co-creator.

KERRI KOBAKOF – "The Creative Collab"

Enter Kerri—aka *CollabWithKerri*—the grounded, genius creative with an eye for aesthetics and a heart for community. Where Nicole brought the fire, Kerri brought the framework. She's the woman who turns chaos into clarity, branding into brilliance, and connection into conversion. With a background in operations, marketing, and the real-world hustle of entrepreneurship, Kerri understood how to turn inspiration into *infrastructure.*

She's the architect behind Exposure Studio and multiple entrepreneurial ventures grounded in collaboration, creativity, and connection. Kerri doesn't just "make it look good"—she makes it mean something. She sees the big picture, ties your story into your strategy, and builds systems that allow your creativity to scale.

Kerri believes in building ecosystems—not just logos. For Kerri, branding isn't about looking like everyone else—it's about owning who you are and creating from a place of alignment.

She's the one who will ask, "What's the purpose behind this?"—and then hand you the roadmap to build it beautifully.

The Birth of a Brand – Our Origin Story
Every movement has a moment. This was ours.

Babes + Business wasn't born in a perfectly curated studio or from a step-by-step business plan. It was born in the mess of motherhood, the chaos of entrepreneurship, and the fire of frustration. It came from two women looking around the rooms they were in, and realizing that *they could build better ones.*

We didn't set out to start a podcast empire; we set out to create *space.* The kind that feels like a deep breath. The kind that makes you sit up straighter. The kind that reflects your truth instead of dimming it.

At first, it was Zoom calls and shared voice notes, dreaming about what could exist if we stopped waiting for permission and started building what we wished existed. We talked about the things no one was saying out loud: the identity crisis of motherhood, the quiet battles of imposter syndrome, the pressure to be perfect, polished, and profitable–*all at once*.

We knew other women were feeling it too. And we were tired of pretending.

That's where Babes + Business was born: at the intersection of real life and radical vision.

From the first episode, we made a vow: no fluff, no filters, just real.

And real doesn't mean messy for the sake of relatability–it means substance. It means strategy *and* soul. It means using the mic not just to share our stories, but to amplify yours.

What started small has since grown into a global network of women building empires, telling truths, and leaving legacies. And it all started with a mic, a mission, and a couple of badass babes who said, *Let's stop playing by the rules. Let's build new ones.*

What Is Babes + Business?

Babes + Business is a podcast, a platform, and a brand visibility playground. Together, Nicole and Kerri built Babes + Business, a movement that's bigger than both of them.

What started as a simple idea––*highlight powerful women doing big things*—quickly grew into a storytelling-driven empire where women weren't just featured... they were *celebrated*. Where business wasn't just about funnels, numbers, and hustle—it was about alignment, legacy, purpose, and community.

It was about creating something that didn't require you to burn out, hide your family life, or lose yourself just to succeed.

It was about being *you:* loudly, boldly, brilliantly.

And that's the mission of Babes + Business:

To spotlight women rewriting the rules, to build a sisterhood that scales with you, and to give you the tools, the stories, and the belief that your path—no matter how unconventional—is valid, worthy, and wildly powerful.

This isn't about chasing someone else's version of success.

This is about defining your own.

And guess what? We're just getting started.

So whether you're here to be inspired, get connected, or take the leap you've been avoiding—welcome, babe.

Why We Started the Podcast

It all began at the table—real conversations, voice notes, creative downloads. The kind of talks that make you go, "Other people need to hear this."

We were seeing brilliant women doing brave things, but too many of them were going unseen, unsupported, or siloed. Women were building businesses but struggling to be visible. They had stories but no platform. They were burnt out from pretending and craving real connection, not just clicks.

We knew we had to do something.

So we pressed record.

And we started talking.

What Makes Babes + Business Different?

We don't do fluff. We don't do facades. And we don't do "just for show."

Every episode is built on truth, trust, and transformation. We create space for the stories that don't get shared on highlight reels, because that's where the real breakthroughs live.

We've had guests cry on mic. We've had guests say, "I've never told anyone this before." That's the power of the space we're building: safe enough to be real, strategic enough to be heard.

Whether you're launching a product, shifting your purpose, scaling your team, or simply craving creative companionship, this is your table.

More Than a Podcast: A Personal Branding Engine

The Babes + Business Podcast is also a platform for visibility.

Every guest gets the HYPE + HEART treatment, because we know how to turn one good conversation into a full-fledged personal brand push.

We help guests create content that aligns with their voice, their vibe, and their values. Professional podcasting, styled photo shoots, branded content clips, and digital media strategy; it's all part of the experience.

We've turned podcast appearances into speaking gigs, media kits, and viral content. Why? Because visibility is strategy. And your voice is your vehicle.

The Power of HYPE + HEART

There are plenty of business podcasts. And plenty of women's groups. What makes us different is the fusion of hype and heart.

We believe in:

- Showing up boldly but also authentically
- Being strategic, but also spirit-led
- Owning the mic, but also passing it to the next babe in line

Our listeners don't just tune in; they transform.

They say "yes" to themselves in a new way.

They pitch that idea. Start that business. Finally post that video.

Because when you see what's possible for someone else, you realize it's possible for you too.

Impact Moments – Stories That Moved Us

Over the years, we've sat across from women who cracked wide open in front of the mic. Women who once whispered their dreams and now shout them from stages. Women who said yes to visibility and found freedom.

There was the single mom who shared how she built her business during naptime—and landed a speaking gig the week her episode dropped.

The survivor who broke her silence on our show, and inspired hundreds to share their own stories for the first time.

The founder who was terrified to show up online—but found her brand voice after listening to women just like her share raw, real truths.

One podcast. Infinite ripple effects.

Because this isn't just content—it's *catalyst*.

It's not just about being featured—it's about being *felt*.

We've had listeners write in to say, "I felt like you were speaking *directly* to me." Or "That episode gave me the courage to quit my job." Or "I finally felt seen."

Those are the metrics we measure.

Not downloads. *Impact*.

Not followers. *Fire*.

Not vanity. *Victory*.

These stories are why we keep going. Because we're not just telling our truth—we're helping other women step into theirs.

Behind the Brand – Our Values

We believe in building from the inside out.

Babes + Business is rooted in five core values:

1. **Authenticity Over Aesthetics:** We love a good brand shoot—but if the message doesn't match the makeup, it's a no for us.
2. **Collaboration Over Competition:** There is room for *all* of us at the table. And if there isn't—we'll build a bigger one.
3. **Strategy + Soul:** We don't believe you should have to choose between feeling aligned and building success. You get both.
4. **Visibility Is Vital:** You can't change lives if no one knows you exist. You deserve to be seen *as you are*.

5. **Power in the Pause:** We value the *quiet* as much as the *hype*. Rest is a strategy. Presence is a superpower.

These values show up in every episode, every event, every brand we touch. This is what makes the Babes + Business movement more than a moment; it's a mission.

Our Future Vision

We didn't build this to be a trend. We built it to be a legacy.

The Babes + Business brand is expanding, and we're just getting started.

From live events and brand-building bootcamps to retreats and creative production spaces like Exposure Studio, we are scaling the mission in every direction: visibility, creativity, connection.

We envision a world where women don't *ask* for space; they *own* it.

Where every woman knows how to tell her story with power, build a brand with integrity, and grow a business that feeds her soul, not just her schedule.

We want to build more stages. More platforms. More opportunities for women to go from invisible to influential.

So whether you're in Naples, Nashville, or New York—this movement has a mic for you.

The question is: are you ready to speak? We are coming to a city near you!

Nicole + Kerri's Unfiltered Advice to Aspiring Entrepreneurs

Nicole Says:

"Don't wait until you feel ready. That version of you that's waiting for the perfect moment? She's not real. You get to start now. Confidence comes from showing up, not thinking about it. You are the strategy. You are the hype. And you are enough."

Kerri Says:

"Start small, but start smart. Branding is more than colors and fonts—it's energy. It's clarity. It's knowing who you are and how you show up. Get obsessed with your purpose, and the rest will follow. Build a brand that *feels* like you and the right people will find you."

Together, We Say:

Show up. Speak up. Scale up.

We're rooting for you—and we built this space for you.

To the Reader:

If you've ever been told you're too much, too loud, too ambitious, this space was built for you.

If you've ever whispered an idea into the dark, hoping someone else had the same thought, we heard you.

And if you've ever wondered if your voice matters, it does.

Babes + Business is more than a podcast.

It's a permission slip.

A spotlight.

So let's slay together.

Let's hit record.

Let's rewrite the rules.

Because when hype meets heart, we all win.

About Nicole & Kerri

Founded by Kerri Kobakof and Nicole Black, *Babes + Business* is more than a podcast—it's a movement. What began as a platform to amplify the voices of female entrepreneurs quickly evolved into a community where bold women build their brands, share their stories, and collaborate without ego. Rooted in the belief that business is better with a little beauty, brains, and badassery, Kerri and Nicole created a space that celebrates ambition, connection, and unapologetic authenticity.

Nicole, "AKA The Hype Lady," is a dynamic speaker, high-energy marketing strategist, and expert in brand storytelling. She empowers clients to find their voice, elevate their confidence, and create magnetic messaging that moves audiences into action. Kerri, known as "The Creative Collab," brings her genius in brand storytelling, media strategy, and content creation. She's the force behind Exposure Studio—Naples' premiere personal branding photography and podcast studio—helping visionaries show up boldly in digital spaces.

Together, they host candid conversations with women who are redefining success—CEOs, creatives, side-hustlers, and startup stars—all showing what's possible when you lead with heart and hustle. Through live events, digital content, and high-impact interviews, *Babes + Business* has become a signature space for rising entrepreneurs to shine.

Whether you're just starting out or scaling your empire, this duo proves that with the right community, collaboration, and a little hype—you don't just grow a brand, you *slay* it!

Instagram:
@babesandbusinesspodcast
@akathehypelady
@collabwithkerri

www.babesandbusinesspodcast.com

Resilient... Here to Lift Others as I Rise

Catherine Backus

I am the second oldest of five children. Growing up, we moved around a lot. My father is a doctor, and his work took us to some incredible places. I spent my formative years living in France and New Zealand—two cultures that shaped my worldview in deep and lasting ways. Constant travel also meant constant change. New schools, new homes, new languages, new friends. I didn't always want to go, but I am grateful for the experiences and lasting friendships I made while living abroad.

Through it all, my siblings and I became very close. We were each other's constants in a life that required frequent adaptation. Our bond was forged not just through shared memories, but shared reinvention. When moving to a new place, before we made friends, we had each other.

Looking back, I see how this early life of movement gave me a unique lens: an ability to connect with anyone, anywhere. It taught me how to read a room, how to listen deeply, and how to appreciate different ways of life and other cultures.

If you know me, I like to say, "I work to travel," and this was instilled in me at a very young age. I travel for the culture, the food, the people, the stories.

While my early life had its adventures, it also had its heartbreaks. I went to college at the University of Florida, where I met my first love. There, we decided to get married right after college and move to Naples, Fla. Soon, that relationship became abusive and toxic, and I thought to myself, "How could I have let this happen? I am a smart, strong, independent woman. How am I allowing someone who says they love me to hurt me?"

I hid my pain and kept it quiet from everyone.

Shortly after we were married, my mother passed away from breast cancer. Losing her was a defining moment for our whole family—one I wasn't emotionally prepared for but one that would shape the rest of my life. My youngest brother was only in eighth grade when she died.

My mother was brilliant. She could have been a CEO of a large company, but chose to dedicate her life to her children and stay home with us. I am grateful for my childhood and the memories I have of us together. Financially, she depended on my father and sacrificed nice things for herself so we could have them. I know my ambition comes from not wanting to rely on a man to take care of me and my drive to be financially independent.

She was fifty-five when she died, and I was twenty-four years old. People always say, "Life is short," but you really don't understand this until you lose someone so close to you. I know death can alienate some families, but I feel it brought my siblings and me closer together. We decided to make more of an effort to see each other as life took us miles apart. My mother would have loved seeing us all together, with all her grandkids. This is what she lived for... family.

Shortly after she died, through the pain and grief, I decided I couldn't continue to stay with my abusive husband. At the time, it felt like another death, and I really could have used my mother to get me through that difficult time, but I think in some ways she gave me the courage to stand up and leave.

Years later, I got a second chance at love and married again. He was my best friend, and we created a wonderful life together. We had trouble conceiving, so after seven years of marriage, we decided to do IVF, which was a grueling, emotional process. We were blessed that it was successful, and we welcomed our daughter Chloe in 2014. She was born with Down syndrome—a reality that changed our lives forever. We had no experience or guidance, and no one to show us the way. She was also born with a heart defect, and I was an emotional wreck, searching for answers. Her early years were filled with a lot of grief, anxiety, endless therapies, and doctors' appointments. I learned that it was OK to mourn the loss of the child and life I thought I was going to have.

I quickly learned how isolating the world is for moms like me—and how important it is to build community around shared experiences.

Gradually, I began connecting with other mothers raising children who have Down syndrome, offering support, sharing resources, and just listening.

As Chloe grew, so did I. I discovered that parenting a child with different abilities isn't about fixing or changing them—it's about shifting my own perspective and celebrating progress, no matter how incremental. Every smile, every word, every step taken was monumental because it was hard-won. Slowly, the grief I once felt made room for fierce pride and gratitude.

Chloe has taught me more about resilience, joy, and unconditional love than any career ever could. She has already changed so many lives for the better, and she's made me an advocate—not just for her, but for every mom silently battling the world for her child's right to be seen, heard, and valued. I wish more than anything that my mother would have had the chance to meet my daughter, Chloe. I know they would have had a special bond.

And just when I thought I'd weathered my share of storms, life reminded me that resilience isn't a destination, but an ongoing practice.

In 2022, Hurricane Ian swept through Southwest Florida, and our home was one of many that were destroyed. Our house flooded, and just like that, years of work, comfort, and stability were washed away.

Afterward, I was oddly calm about it. I was probably in shock, but I felt that as long as we were safe and Chloe was healthy, to me, that was all that mattered. We love Naples and our life here, so we rebuilt our home. Our community, friends, church, and co-workers all rose to help us clean out the house. It was a very humbling experience. When everything you own is at the curb for garbage, you realize that we all have way too much stuff. Losing photos of my mom and grandparents was tough, but memories matter more—people are what's truly important. God keeps showing me everything is out of my control—a hard thing to accept, and I still struggle with it.

Each time life knocked me down, I found small miracles in community, in kindness, and in the courage to begin again. This is resilience.

Today, I'm navigating another major life change: another divorce. It's not something I ever imagined for my life, but after 18 years of marriage, my best friend, my family, Chloe's father, and I tried to make it work for Chloe. But in the end, God seems to have other plans for me.

Getting knocked down teaches you to recover quickly. I choose this time to grieve, heal, and become a better version of myself. This was yet again another time in my life where I needed my mother more than ever, but I had to become my own best friend, my own cheerleader.

There were days when the weight of loss pressed in so heavily, I could barely catch my breath, and nights when hope felt too far away. Instead of shrinking from the pain, I leaned into it. I worked on forgiveness, and I chose to focus not on what I've lost, but what I've learned. Not on what didn't work, but on who I've become in the process.

I want other women to know that it's okay to start over—again and again if necessary. Reinvention isn't failure; it's freedom.

While life was happening, I was trying to hustle in my real estate career. I've moved from simply selling homes to leading teams, training new agents, and mentoring younger women entering the business. Real estate can be a cutthroat world, but I try to lead differently—with empathy, strategy, honesty, and fun.

I remind new agents that you can be successful without losing your soul. That you can make money *and* make a difference.

I've rebuilt after loss, made mistakes, learned, and kept going. Real estate is my profession, but I don't just help people buy and sell houses. I am a part of people's stories—new beginnings, marriages, babies, divorces, deaths, floods, fresh starts. I am a trusted guide during some of their hardest and happiest moments. Real estate is a relationship business, and with everything I have been through, it has been my relationships with community, friends, and colleagues that have helped me through it all.

We don't always get to choose our circumstances, but we do get to choose our response. And my response—through grief, motherhood, natural disasters, and divorce—has always been this: This journey of life—of rebuilding, of redefining success, of living and loving through uncertainty—has taught me that joy is an act of courage.

Keep going. Keep loving. Keep building. And leave the world softer than you found it.

About Catherine

Catherine Backus is a dynamic and compassionate force in Southwest Florida real estate, serving as the team lead of The Omni Group at Compass.

Catherine earned a bachelor's degree in real estate from the University of Florida's Warrington School of Business with a focus on finance, economics, and new construction. She is a real estate broker sales associate and has experience selling for both custom and production builders throughout Southwest Florida. She has sold over one thousand homes throughout SW Florida. With a career built on resilience, empathy, and a drive to uplift others, Catherine leads with both strategy and heart—empowering her clients and team through every transition, from first homes to forever homes.

She is honored to serve as the Women of Compass Naples Ambassador, where she advocates for greater connection, mentorship, and representation among women in real estate. As a member of Compass Plus, a specialized division of Compass, Catherine helps older adults and their families navigate major life changes with dignity, grace, and personalized care.

A dedicated mother to a daughter with Down syndrome, Catherine brings fierce advocacy and lived experience to every role she holds—offering a voice to those who often feel unseen. Whether she's mentoring new agents, guiding families through emotional sales, or helping seniors downsize with compassion, Catherine's work is rooted in one mission: to serve with purpose, elevate others, and leave every person better than she found them.

Instagram: @catsells239
www.theomnigroupre.com

The Dreamer Who Dared to Design Her Own Path

Elizabeth Cinquini

The very first world I designed didn't have walls. No floorplans, no wallpaper, not a single piece of furniture. It lived entirely in my mind—saturated in color, overflowing with curiosity and endless possibility.

I grew up an only child in Brooklyn, New York. No siblings. No chaos. Just me and a wildly vivid imagination. While other kids played with their brothers and sisters, I was busy dreaming about the faraway places I wanted to explore, the life I wanted to create, and all the magic I knew one day I'd experience.

From the outside, I seemed quiet and shy—the observer. But inside, I was filled with ideas and vision. The people around me didn't dream like that, they didn't get it, so I learned early on to keep it to myself.

"You live in a dream world," my parents used to say, half-annoyed, half-concerned. And they were right. I did.

What they didn't realize at the time was ... that wasn't a flaw. It was my superpower.

I'd cut out inspiration photos from magazines and tape them to my wall. I was making collages before I even knew what a vision board was. I was creating my future.

The world tells us to be practical. To fit in. But what we really need are more dreamers—those brave enough to build what they can't yet see.

That little girl—the dreamer, the manifester–didn't need applause or support. As an only child, she learned to believe in herself from within.

Growing up alone gave me the courage to explore, adapt, and keep going until I found what fit. But the quiet, reserved version of me? I had to unlearn her to leave my mark on the world.

I've changed careers, traveled the world alone, graduated college, gone back to school, worked corporate jobs, quit corporate jobs, taken more classes than I can count, started a business, and hired mentors. A friend once teased, "How many certifications do you need?" But to me, staying curious is how you keep evolving and turning dreams into reality.

Maybe your inner dreamer is still quietly waiting. Your dreams aren't silly—they're sacred whispers from the life you're meant to live.

For years, I thought I was shy. But it wasn't shyness; it was disconnection.

I didn't feel seen or understood. The conversations happening around me didn't spark anything in me. The people didn't light me up. So I stayed on the outside—imagining a different world. Now I know better: change the room, change the people.

After high school, I left New York to attend college out of state, without a single familiar face. Even at seventeen, I was ready for a fresh start—never concerned with following the crowd.

After graduation, I moved back to New York City to start a career in fashion magazines. I loved parts of it, but deep down, it wasn't the dream.

So I took fashion design classes at night while working full-time. The creativity lit me up, but something still didn't fit.

Then one day, I saw a job posting. I didn't have the experience, but my gut said it was meant for me. I saw myself in that role before it happened. I didn't know it then, but that was manifestation.

I got the job as corporate visual merchandising assistant for a global brand. Soon after, I became manager of visual merchandising, worldwide. I was twenty-three.

I loved it. Designing stores, leading teams, traveling. I'll never forget watching our new flagship store in Hawaii come alive. I started noticing people's reactions to my work, and that's when I realized: my imagination could move people.

But the path wasn't smooth. There were setbacks. Tears. Counterproductive coworkers. Long hours. Unrealistic deadlines. Eventually, the company was sold, and that dream job turned into a nightmare. It was time for me to go.

One of my superpowers? Knowing when something no longer feels right—and having the courage to walk away. I've left jobs, ended partnerships, cut ties with friends and even family who didn't align anymore with the life I was building. My mom once said, "How do you cut people off like that? You're coldhearted." But I don't see it as cold; it's clarity.

I'm either all in—or I'm out. That's my other superpower. It keeps me focused, evolving, and raising the bar, grateful for every dream I've checked off, and manifesting the next.

After nearly a decade in corporate design, I launched my own design firm in 2015: Elizabeth Cinquini Interiors. I had no business plan, no roadmap—just determination and intuition.

And it worked. Word spread. Projects came in. I became known for custom homes and remodels. I loved my clients and the creative freedom.

But not every client was a dream. One couple seemed nice, until the husband berated his wife during our first session. In public. In front of their kids. Horrified, I realized this was their "norm." If he spoke to her like that, there was no way he'd respect me. I should've walked away then. But I didn't. I was shocked, unsure how to handle something I'd never experienced before. Their behavior spiraled: harassment, lies, threats, unpaid invoices. Eventually, I cut ties for good.

It was a nightmare—but also a turning point that taught me to trust my gut, screen every client, and say no without guilt.

In 2021, I had my best year in business, but I was burned out.

New York City—once my inspiration—was draining me instead. I knew I couldn't grow there anymore.

So in 2022, my husband, kids, and I packed up and moved to Naples, Fla. We only visited once on vacation. We didn't know a soul.

We traded chaos for calm. Skyscrapers for palm trees. And the moment we arrived, I felt it—a deep, full-body exhale.

Waking up to blue skies and sunshine every day changes you. It softens you. It reminds you that life doesn't have to be so hard. I feel an overwhelming sense of peace here. We really do live in paradise now.

But starting over? That's hard.

No friends. No clients. People warned me: Naples is a tough town for a new business. It'll take years.

They were right. At first, I was chasing opportunities, trying to prove myself. Then I stopped. I chose to be more selective— about the rooms, the relationships, and the clients. The right people will find me.

Three years in, slowly they are. People tell me, "We love your style because it's different. Naples needs you." So I keep going.

It's been anything but easy. I've been burned by both business associates and friendships I once trusted. I worked with a business I later discovered was taking advantage of their vendors and clients. I wasn't paid and lost a great client in the process, but I spoke up and called the owner out on their lies. The business eventually closed and the owner disappeared. Another hard-earned lesson.

Then came a betrayal that cut even deeper. People we once trusted hurt our family in unthinkable ways, and we had no choice but to cut all ties and let the legal process run its course.

Both of these experiences left scars, some emotional, some physical. But they also made me sharper, wiser, and fiercely protective. They taught me to enforce boundaries and ignited a fire to fight for my family, myself, and the business I've poured my heart into.

Now, I'm carving my own lane in Naples—on my own terms, with a voice, vision, and approach that's entirely mine.

No, I don't have it all figured out. But I'm building. I'm becoming.

And I wouldn't change a thing.

While writing this chapter, an incredible partnership opportunity appeared out of the blue. Manifestation is real. Will it be a breakthrough... or a bust? I don't know, but I'm excited to go through the process. Follow along on this journey with me to see how it all turns out.

Every twist, every heartbreak, every doubt—it's all part of the design. Life doesn't move in a straight line. The magic is in who you become after the setbacks and failures.

Even if you feel it's not working, it is. You're learning. You're growing. You're planting seeds. Just keep going.

Our stories are our superpower. No one else can live it, write it, or design it for you.

And if you've ever felt like the outsider, the quiet one, the underestimated one—just know: you're in good company.

The girl I used to be taught me everything—how to dream, trust myself, and keep going no matter what life throws my way.

I carry her with me—into every room, every project, every new version of me.

I'm also a mom to two incredible teenagers, and if they learn one thing from me, I hope it's this: Dream big. Rise stronger. And design a life on your own terms because that is the ultimate freedom.

The real success? A life that doesn't just look good—but feels good. That's how you leave your mark.

About Elizabeth

Elizabeth Cinquini is a bold creative, soulful visionary, and the founder of Elizabeth Cinquini Interiors—a full-service interior design firm specializing in custom homes and luxury renovations. With a background in corporate design, visual merchandising, and fashion, Elizabeth built a thriving design business in New York City before following her intuition and relocating to Naples, Florida, to design a new kind of life—one filled with beauty, balance, and brave decisions.

Born and raised in Brooklyn as an only child, Elizabeth's imagination was her first blueprint. Her quiet, intuitive nature shaped a fearless ability to dream and reinvent. From fashion magazines to flagship store design to launching her own firm, Elizabeth's path has been anything but linear—and that's what makes her story so powerful. She's not afraid to pivot, to start over, or to bet on herself.

Known for her timeless, soul-filled interiors and concierge-level service, Elizabeth believes that design is more than just how a home looks—it's how it makes you feel. Her mission is to give busy professionals and families their time back, while transforming their homes into deeply personal sanctuaries.

Whether she's creating spaces, writing, traveling, or mentoring other creatives, Elizabeth brings a signature mix of intuition, elegance, and depth to everything she touches.

Her work has been featured in several publications. But her greatest success has been designing a life she truly loves while inspiring others to do the same.

www.elizabethcinquini.com
Instagram: @elizabethcinquini
Facebook: Elizabeth Cinquini Interiors

Building a Legacy
Jessica Diaz

In *Slaying Southwest Florida*, I shared the grit it took to rebuild my life: raising four children on my own, launching a real estate career from scratch, and turning every challenge into an opportunity. That chapter was about survival. This one is about expansion—about building legacy, deepening connection, and leaving a mark that matters.

For years, I poured myself into my kids and my work. Love wasn't even on the table; I told myself I was fine without it. Then Thom came along—not to complete me, but to match me. He brought his own dreams, his own fire, and together we discovered that partnership isn't about losing yourself—it's about multiplying what's possible. Our relationship wasn't some fairytale rescue; it was a meeting of equals, a merging of two strong individuals who decided to build something greater together. Thom's support has been a powerful force, allowing me to keep pushing boundaries in my career and personal life.

This past year, we celebrated two of our sons' weddings—one in the olive groves of Italy, another on the crystal shores of Lake Tahoe. These weren't just celebrations; they were moments that opened our eyes to the beauty of blending families and cultures, of legacy in motion. These events gave Thom and me a glimpse of the future we are building together—a future rich with shared adventures, deep bonds, and family milestones. Now, as we plan our own wedding, we look forward to continuing this journey together.

Naples's luxury market is as demanding as it is rewarding. My clients expect precision, creativity, and heart—and that's what I deliver. This past year, I worked while traveling through Scotland, Norway, Ireland, Spain, Italy, Switzerland, and Dubai. Mornings might begin negotiating a contract; afternoons might find me wandering historic streets or absorbing the local culture. Traveling sharpens me. It forces me to adapt, to see things from different perspectives, and it fuels my creativity. When I return home, I bring that fresh energy to every client interaction and every listing. I understand that buying or selling a luxury home is not just a transaction—it's a deeply personal chapter in someone's life story. My ability to connect the dots between global inspiration and local expertise has been key to my momentum.

Every country I visited offered a unique lesson. Scotland, with its rugged landscapes and resilient spirit, reminded me that strength comes from enduring storms. Ireland's warmth and simple pleasures reinforced the importance of finding joy in everyday moments. Spain and Italy, steeped in history and passion, taught me that authenticity and heritage enrich our lives and homes. But it was Dubai that truly crystallized a vision for me—standing at the edge of the Burj Al Arab, one of the world's most iconic and luxurious hotels, I felt a surge of possibility. That moment wasn't about indulgence; it was about recognizing how faith, hard work, and bold vision converge to create extraordinary outcomes. It was a powerful reminder that no matter where we come from, persistence can carry us to heights we once only dreamed of.

My heart has always held a vision of a large, loving family gathered around a table—candles flickering, stories flowing freely, a place where everyone feels seen and cherished. Now, blending our eight children into one family is the beautiful, lively reality of that vision. It's a work in progress, with all the challenges and joys that come with merging histories and personalities. That same nurturing, inclusive energy drives my business philosophy. I'm passionate about mentoring new agents, hosting women's networking events, and creating spaces—both physical and emotional—where others can thrive. For me, legacy isn't about possessions or accolades. It's about the faith, love, and inspiration we pass down, creating ripples that touch generations beyond our own.

Independence gave me grit; partnership gave me wings. Thom is building his own brand with the same passion I bring to real estate, and together we amplify each other's strengths.

We're not just growing careers—we're shaping a future grounded in shared purpose and aligned values. The hustle of the luxury market and the demands of our blended family require teamwork, communication, and unwavering support. We celebrate each other's wins, navigate setbacks with grace, and stay focused on what matters most: building a legacy of love, resilience, and impact.

My mark will be measured in people, not numbers: my children carrying forward faith and resilience; the women I mentor finding their voices; the clients whose homes become the backdrop of their biggest dreams. I want every woman reading this to know that your story is your power. Whether you're in survival mode or expansion mode, every chapter holds purpose. Claim your narrative. Shape it boldly. And let your influence echo through generations, building legacies that inspire and uplift.

About Jessica

Jessica Diaz is a Naples-based luxury real estate advisor who believes success is born from vision, persistence, and compassion. Since 2013, she has built a top-producing career while raising four children as a single mother, transforming obstacles into stepping stones.

Jessica has combined business with exploration—traveling the world—while expanding her presence in the luxury market. Alongside her fiancé and their blended family of eight children, she is committed to building a legacy rooted in faith, resilience, and impact.

Jessica mentors emerging agents, organizes women's networking events, and curates client experiences that celebrate life's milestones. Her mission is to empower women to own their narratives, pursue their ambitions unapologetically, and create legacies that extend far beyond themselves.

www.diazsells.com
Instagram: @luxelifestyleswfl

Fighting for the Little Girl behind You

Talisha Faber

I'm excited to write this chapter in *Slaying Naples*.

First, thank you to all the women who have inspired me to be more open, to share more of my story, and to really understand what it means to lift my arms. Before *Slaying Southwest Florida*, I do believe I was in hiding. Feeling somewhat exposed, I shared how I came to my faith through this little white church bus. Although that little white church bus couldn't solve all my problems, the faith I learned at that age helped me work through many of them.

Here's my story—the part I don't usually share—that I hope will inspire others to stop hiding.

I had my second real boyfriend, who I thought was my "true love," when this happened. I'm going to call him Johnny (not his real name). At the young age of nineteen, I caught him cheating. At that time, I'd been having a hate-hate relationship with myself. With everyone on the magazine covers being the size of Kate Moss, at ninety-one pounds, I definitely wasn't model material. And even though I thought I had a pretty badass dance career and had started working at a major supermarket chain, I was completely oblivious to who I was and what I had to offer.

(I know many of us still feel like we're nineteen and stuck in that space—which is exactly why I decided to share this part of my story.)

I walked to Johnny's house one day, only to see his old girlfriend standing there in a little white nightshirt that looked like it belonged to my boyfriend. She was clearly surprised to see me at the door. After stepping inside and seeing what was happening, I left. I was heartbroken and completely lost about how to deal with those emotions.

That day, I went to the local supermarket where I worked, bought razor blades, grabbed a handful of pills, and went home to my two-bedroom apartment, where my roommate was in the next room. And I tried to end my life.

My roommate at the time, Jody—bless her heart—had no idea what I was going through or what was about to happen. My cry for help came, but it came with some big realizations.

The first realization: You don't get shoelaces when you're in the mental ward.

The second: You have zero access to your friends and family.

A song by Lisa Loeb played, and I cried, listening to it over and over in remembrance of Johnny. I knew I'd get his attention this way. Call it manipulative. Call it awful. Call it ugly. I call it depression and hurt. I had zero tools to work through it in my younger years.

My uncle had died by suicide. I knew how hurtful and painful that had been for my family, especially for my father, who was in the next room when it happened. But in that moment, I couldn't see how my pain could possibly impact anyone else.

I write this because I believe it's something many of us are familiar with: when you're in the middle of that kind of funk you can't seem to shake, your mind can go in any direction.

Many people will be shocked by this story. To be honest, it didn't end with just that one attempt. It ended after several attempts—and after finally gaining the right tools to address the issues I was trying to resolve in a heartbroken state.

Since then, I haven't experienced a suicidal thought—praise Jesus. But I also praise the medical staff, my family, and the people who continued to lift my arms when I couldn't lift them myself.

Faith is powerful. I believe it can change those thoughts if you're able to see Him and hear Him. At some of those lowest moments, I couldn't see or hear anything. If you feel lost or broken, please know: it doesn't have to end like that. Ending your life continues the devastation by deeply hurting those you leave behind.

To this day, I've never spoken to my dad or family about those attempts. I assume, by this chapter—and as my tears fall while writing—that it's not forgotten. That torturous time I put them through left an impact.

I often talk about ripple effects. The ripple effect of my understanding that level of depression—the feeling of not being able to see above the water—gives me the power to speak to others who are in the midst of devastation and despair. I hope I provide hope. I hope I can lift your arms. And if I'm not capable, I hope someone sees you like they saw me—and does it for you.

Today, as a single, full-time mom raising two teenagers—and having brought another teen into my home as a volunteer—I've served and loved in our communities in tremendous ways. I do this because I remember that feeling of hopelessness, and I will never forget it.

As the economic development officer at the largest credit union in Florida, and as a commercial real estate broker who works with an amazing team of highly professional humans, I'm honored to say that we—together—walk to support the American Foundation for Suicide Prevention.

I walk in honor of my Uncle Pete.

I walk to honor the families who don't have the story I do.

If you feel lost, depressed, defeated, unlovable, tarnished, broken—I will say this: We belong together. All of us.

Regardless of the accolades, the awards, or the world-renowned movements, you have the power to make changes—in your life, in your outcomes, and in your opportunities. The biggest investment you can make is in yourself. And if I could tell my younger self anything, I'd say: "One day, you will be fighting for the little girl behind you."

I remember the overwhelming mix of shame, isolation, and confusion in those cold, sterile walls. The silence felt louder than anything I'd ever experienced. You feel forgotten, like the world is continuing outside and you've been paused. You start to wonder if you're more broken than you thought. But there's also something else—clarity. A terrifying kind of stillness that gives you a chance to see your pain from the outside looking in.

For anyone reading this who may be feeling overwhelmed, please know: you are not alone, and there is help.

National Suicide & Crisis Lifeline: 988

You can call or text 988 anytime to talk to someone who cares.

Thank you to Leigh Clark for allowing me to be exposed in all of this. There are many stories I could share, but I felt in my heart that this is the one that needed the most exposure.

I'm grateful.

About Talisha

Talisha Faber currently serves as the economic development officer at Suncoast Credit Union, where she leads statewide initiatives focused on workforce development, affordable housing, and sustainable community growth. A trusted leader across Florida, Talisha works to build strong partnerships that drive economic mobility and expand access to financial resources for individuals, families, veterans, and small businesses.

With over two decades of experience in financial services, commercial real estate, and community impact, Talisha has built a reputation for delivering results while keeping people at the heart of her mission. Her background includes years as a senior vice president and commercial lender/private client director at leading financial institutions, as well as a successful career as a commercial real estate advisor, where she has loved working with investors, as well as blue collar trades.

Alongside her professional work, Talisha is a dynamic speaker known for connecting with women's groups, business leaders, and nonprofit partners. She is especially passionate about advocating for children, veterans initiatives, trade and workforce opportunities, and affordability.

A native Floridian, Talisha's nonprofit involvement is extensive and heartfelt—serving on several boards in Southwest Florida, many that support entrepreneurship, children, grief, and loss, as well as suicide prevention.

Talisha was a recipient of the prestigious 2023 Women of Distinction Award given to her by Congressman Byron Donalds and recognized as one of the Top 100 Women to Know in Florida. She is also a host volunteer mom with Better Together and was recognized for her humanitarian work with SVN International's 2024 Humanitarian of the Year Award.

Talisha has received many accolades for her work for hurricane victims and continues to lead with heart on many "outside the box" initiatives through her work with affordable housing and workforce development. Talisha is also a proud mom to two teenagers, and a regular volunteer at her local church and food bank alongside her father.

Instagram: @Talishaconnects
LinkedIn: Talisha Faber

She Didn't Just Heal—She Built an Empire

Sofia L. Gonzalez

Most people saw the brand. The growth. The awards. The strategy. But what they didn't see was the healing.

They didn't see the girl who had to fight to believe she was worthy of softness. The woman who built her business while carrying unspoken grief. The faith it took to keep showing up when all she really wanted was to feel safe enough to be seen.

The truth is, I didn't just build a brand. I rebuilt myself.

Most people know me as the co-founder of *Affluence Media Agency and* Founder of *The Healed Babe.*

But I am just Sofia L. Gonzalez. There's so much more than the titles. Before the platforms, before the global stages and strategy decks, there was a girl who had to learn that healing doesn't disqualify you. It qualifies you to lead from a place the world rarely teaches: *presence.*

There was a season where I looked whole on the outside. But inside, I was silently unraveling.

Still, I led. I built. I delivered. Not because I wanted to disappear, but because I longed to be fully seen. And that's what healing gave me. Not a perfect version of myself, but an honest one. Not a shiny brand, but a sacred assignment. Not just results, but revelation.

Because when I stopped performing and started healing, everything changed. I no longer had to chase visibility. I became it. Not through noise. Through clarity. Through softness. Through stillness. Through truth.

Eventually, I got the chance to pause. But not at first.

When my father passed, the grief came suddenly. I remember the call. The panic. The moment I couldn't find my keys because my hands were shaking too hard. I was trying to get to the hospital and praying it would be like the other times. But this time, it wasn't.

I cried. I grieved.

There I was, standing on the edge of despair, trying to come to terms with my father's passing. But in the midst of it all, life was offering opportunities.

I had just become a seven-time best-selling author—with a three-time Hot New Release on Amazon for my co-authorship of *RISE UP: Women Who Lead Building Legacy*. That moment opened a door I could have only dreamed of: an invitation to speak at the First Ladies Forum Economic Development Summit in Dubai.

My family was so proud. Especially my parents. My father always told me to go after everything God has for me. But the summit in Dubai was scheduled for just five days after he passed.

I was conflicted. Torn between duty and destiny. Grief and greatness. How could I leave when I hadn't even fully processed the loss? And yet, deep down, I knew the truth: My father would have wanted me to go. He would've told me to get on that plane. So I did. I boarded that flight carrying more than just luggage. I carried the weight of my grief and the weight of my calling.

And I stood there, on that stage in Dubai, heartbroken but whole in purpose. Smiling through the ache. Speaking through the silence. Honoring him with every word, even though my heart was still catching up. When I came back home, I didn't slow down. I kept building, creating, producing, and performing. I was achieving, but I hadn't exhaled. Not fully. Eventually, I gave myself permission to pause.

Hawaii gave me that. Not just a vacation but sacred stillness.

It was the first time I allowed myself to stop performing and simply be. I gave myself permission to breathe, to explore, to say yes to the parts of me I had tucked away—or never met. I gave myself permission to know what it feels like to be alone and not be lonely. I started writing my first book. I stood in front of cameras and remembered what it felt like to feel beautiful again. I modeled. I dated. I won a dance battle at an NBA halftime game. I climbed mountains, cried on beaches, made new friends, and let the ocean hold the pain I had buried.

I grieved my dad for real this time.

And when I came back to Southwest Florida, I came home a different woman. Not because life got easier, but because I had shifted. What I walked into required the most anchored, healed, and discerning version of me. Hawaii didn't fix everything. But it reminded me of who I was beneath it all.

Because when I finally gave myself permission to pause, something shifted. Not overnight. Not all at once. But slowly, quietly, and deeply.

I started healing not by stepping away from everything, but by showing up differently. Less to be seen and more to be present. Less from urgency... and more from alignment.

I didn't stop performing immediately. But I did start noticing the parts of me that longed to be held, not just applauded. And that's where the real healing began.

I didn't just heal. I built an empire from it.

And now, I help other women do the same through strategy, yes, but also through soul.

Because branding without healing is just performance. And I'm not here to *perform*. I'm here to *embody*.

I lead two brands. Not because I set out to wear multiple hats, but because both visions were born from different parts of me. Affluence Media Agency came from clarity, from structure, from a desire to elevate how brands show up in the world with precision and presence. The Healed Babe came from surrender. From softness. From the sacred need to heal out loud and create space for other women to do the same.

They may seem like two different worlds, but to me, they're deeply connected.

At Affluence, we help high-end service brands refine their message, elevate their visuals, and align their operations so they can grow with elegance and intention. My sister Evita leads the systems. I lead the story. Together, we build with excellence, merging strategy and beauty in a way that feels seamless, sophisticated, and scalable.

At The Healed Babe, I speak from the part of me that broke open and found God in the pieces. It's where I create. It's where I cry sometimes. It's where I remind women that healing isn't just about overcoming. It's about returning. Returning to softness. To identity. To the truth that you are already whole, even while you're still becoming.

Both brands are a reflection of who I am. One sharp. One soft. One built for strategy. One built from story. Both born from healing.

This season of my life isn't just about building. It's about claiming who I am and walking into who I'm becoming as if I am already her. The highest, healed version of myself that I dream of, and helping others do the same.

God has been refining how I lead, how I show up, how I speak, how I move. Not from ambition but from alignment. I no longer lead from urgency or pressure. I lead from discernment. From presence. From the deep, grounded knowing that I am already her. Not because I've arrived. But because I remember.

I remember the girl who doubted her voice. The woman who smiled through storms. The daughter who once felt too broken to lead. And I honor her. I look for her in others, so I can hold space for their healing, too. Because she's the reason I lead the way I do now.

Now, I lead with softness. I honor alignment, and when it's not present, I choose sacred boundaries. I lead with bold yeses and unapologetic no's. Even when it's messy, I anchor myself in elegance and strategy—not just with emotion, but with God at the center of it all.

Because legacy isn't just about what I build. It's about how I show up while building it.

I didn't just heal. I came home to myself. And from that place, I've created a life and a calling that reflects every version of the woman I've had to fight to become.

This isn't the end of the story; it's just the beginning. But this time, I'm not chasing success. I'm embodying wholeness.

I am her now. Still becoming. Already whole. Crowned and called.

The Healed Babe's Way

Practices. Postures. Reminders for the woman becoming.

Healing doesn't happen all at once. It happens in whispers; in daily decisions, in quiet returns to truth, in the gentle remembering of who you are. This next part isn't a checklist. It's not a blueprint. It's a rhythm. A heart posture. A way of moving through the world when you've chosen to live healed.

These are the anchors I return to when I feel ungrounded. They are reminders that I don't have to strive, prove, or perform. They're not rules, they're sacred truths for the woman becoming. For the woman who leads with both softness and strength. For the woman who knows that healing isn't about fixing, it's about *remembering.*

Because you don't need to be louder. You just need to be anchored.

Here are seven reminders I return to—daily, gently, honestly:

1. Wholeness is not earned. It's remembered.
You don't have to become anything to be worthy. You already are.
Affirmation: I am whole, even while I'm still unfolding. I don't have to chase what I've already been given.
Scripture: "You are complete in Him." — Colossians 2:10

2. Softness is strength.
You don't have to harden to survive. You get to lead with softness and conviction.
Affirmation: My softness is not a liability. It's my power reclaimed. I lead with both grace and truth.

Scripture: "Let your gentleness be evident to all. The Lord is near." — Philippians 4:5

3. Boundaries are holy.
You are not difficult for protecting your peace. You are discerning. Sacred things aren't always accessible.
Affirmation: I am allowed to say no without guilt. My peace is worth preserving.
Scripture: "Above all else, guard your heart, for everything you do flows from it." — Proverbs 4:23

4. Your body is not your enemy.
It is not too much. It is not the problem. It is not shameful. It is sacred.
Affirmation: My body is the temple where God dwells. I honor it, not from fear, but from love.
Scripture: "Do you not know that your bodies are temples of the Holy Spirit?" — 1 Corinthians 6:19

5. You can be strategic and spirit-led.
Your intuition is not separate from wisdom. Both can live in your leadership.
Affirmation: I follow divine strategy. I trust both my insight and God's timing.
Scripture: "The steps of a good woman are ordered by the Lord." — Psalm 37:23

6. Rest is not weakness.
You are allowed to slow down without losing momentum. Rest is how you rise well. Affirmation: I am not behind. I am in rhythm with grace. My rest is worship.
Scripture: "In repentance and rest is your salvation, in quietness and trust is your strength." — Isaiah 30:15

7. You don't have to chase visibility.
You don't need to perform to be seen. Your presence speaks when you're aligned.

Affirmation: I don't have to strive to be seen. The right doors will recognize what God has placed within me.

Scripture: "A woman who fears the Lord is to be praised... her works will bring her praise at the city gate." — Proverbs 31:30–31

Before You Go

If you've made it this far, maybe something stirred in you.

Maybe you see your story in mine. Maybe you're in your unraveling. Maybe you're rising again. Maybe you're still remembering who you are.

Wherever you are, I honor you.

You don't have to have it all figured out. You just have to be willing to come home to yourself. Again and again. Softly. Boldly. Faithfully.

You're not late. You're right on time. You're not too much. You're more than enough.

You're not becoming her. You already are.

The Healed Babe.

About Sofia

Sofia L. Gonzalez is a globally recognized luxury brand strategist, creative visionary, and founder whose work sits at the intersection of healing, elegance, and high-impact leadership.

@thehealedbabe on Instagram, TikTok, and YouTube
Step into your healing, wholeness, and identity. Shop the brand, watch the journey, and join the community.
www.thehealedbabe.com
For brand elevation and luxury growth: Visit www.affluencemediaagency.com to explore how we help legacy-driven brands refine their visuals, messaging, and digital operations for sustainable success.

I Am Statement Peace

Jessy Lee

I've been reading rooms my whole life.

I come from a background that shaped me to anticipate the needs of others, to overperform, and to keep peace where there was none. As a child, I stayed safe by sensing people's energy, picking up on changes in tone or movement, and knowing when to speak or remain silent. My nervous system was made for survival, not happiness, yet in that state, I began to create something new. At first, it looked like hyper-independence. Little did I know it would be the root system of my power.

Later, hospitality became the place where I refined it. Where I took what I already knew and turned it into something I could use.

Reading people, anticipating needs, staying three steps ahead—this all came naturally. I could walk into any room, and with a single scan, I could tell you exactly what everyone needed—whether they were happy, satisfied, annoyed, or ready to leave.

That people-pleasing instinct—this gift I picked up from a childhood that required it—became a superpower I still carry today.

But even as I was rising in the hospitality world, I knew I'd hit a ceiling. I'd learned everything I was meant to learn there.

And that matched the knowing I'd been carrying since I was a kid: I was made for more.

That knowing followed me everywhere. I carried this feeling in my bones like I had big work to do, and whatever I was doing at the time wasn't it. The hardest part? I had no idea what *it* was yet. So, the void remained.

I kept wondering when it would finally show up. And the longer it took, the more impatient I became.

People love to say things like, *"The universe will reveal your purpose when the time is right."* But when you already know you're meant for something more—and it hasn't shown up yet—those words start to wear thin.

The moment Statement Peace was born, I was deep in the middle of life, raising a baby, pregnant with another, no sleep, no space. And still, I remember that moment like it happened yesterday.

I was sitting on my living room floor, surrounded by the noise of motherhood, holding a piece I had just made. I lifted it up toward the sky and said out loud, *I'm going to put this everywhere.*

And I meant it.

It wasn't ego. It wasn't wishful thinking. It was a knowing. The same knowing I'd carried since I was a kid. It had finally shown up in my hands.

But here's the truth about having a vision like that: it's lonely.

Trying to explain your vision to someone who doesn't see it is exhausting. My husband, a numbers man and a brilliant businessman in his own right, looked at what I was building and called it a hobby. Not maliciously. Just practically. He couldn't see the margins. He didn't get the vision. He wanted proof.

And that stung, because I finally felt like I'd found what I'd been searching for all along. My calling. My craft. My purpose. But in his eyes, it didn't hold value because it wasn't generating money.

That was the gut punch.

And that's where it shifted for me. That's when I stopped trying to prove everyone else wrong and started proving myself right.

And honestly, that's one of the hardest parts. You're not just building a business—you're trying to be understood.

I was out there doing everything I could to get it moving in the first year. Cold calls. Rejections. Getting hung up on over and over again. I was desperate for someone to say, "*I see it, I feel it, you're brilliant.*" I wanted that outside validation so badly.

But looking back, I know now it wasn't just about the work I was doing. It was about how I was showing up. The vibration was thirsty.

Everything changed when I started learning about epigenetics. About how our bodies hold onto everything: old stories, survival patterns, the things we think we've outgrown but haven't.

That's when it hit me. I needed to not only see it; I needed to feel it in every cell of my body.

Manifestation isn't about vision boards or writing goals in a journal. It's about becoming the version of you who already has what she's working for. It's about showing up like it's already done.

I stopped waiting for proof. I stopped waiting for permission. I started moving like I already had it—because deep down, I knew I did. I wasn't hoping anymore. I was certain.

And everything around me started to shift, too.

Orders started coming in. People started buying.

And not only was that validating for me, but it also gave my husband the "proof" he needed to finally see it as viable.

And honestly, once it became viable to him, the expansion pushed even further.

But there was something else happening too, a pattern was forming.

When I was creating, I felt happy. And when I felt happy, I felt grateful. And when I was grateful, everything around me felt abundant.

It wasn't just about the jewelry anymore. It was about the state I was in when I created it.

When I was tapped into gratitude, truly connected with my life, the ideas came easier. The doors opened faster. The right people showed up. The validation I'd been chasing suddenly landed at my feet.

It was like I became a conduit. A channel. I could feel the ideas streaming in like I wasn't even trying to create; I was just *receiving*.

And from that space, Statement Peace kept expanding. Not all at once—but naturally, steadily—because I was finally moving from a place of flow, not force.

Statement Peace grew as I grew. The more I healed old wounds and the more I trusted myself, the more aligned the business became.

And those doors that were opening weren't just in my neighborhood or my state—they were across the country. Then across oceans. I started seeing my creations land in shops and homes all over the world—in Switzerland, in Paris, in small European villages, and even in bustling cities I'd never even stepped foot in.

The vibration traveled farther than I imagined. Because when something is built from a real place—with authenticity, intention, and love—it's undeniable.

So, I kept going. I kept creating. I kept becoming.

I've shipped to thousands of stores by now, but I'll never forget that first "yes"—and the way it felt. I call on that feeling often to tap back into gratitude when I lose the way.

Every mantra I carve, every piece I design, every offering I bring into the world is a reflection of the work I've done to remember who I am. To trust myself. To show up raw, real, and authentic. I didn't wait for the industry to open a door—I built my own. And then I held it open for others.

That's the legacy. That's the vibration. That's the revolution.

I didn't just become a brand. I became a mirror for every woman who forgot she was already enough. For every mother, every maker, every dreamer who wonders if it's too late or too messy or too far out of reach. It's not. You just need to see it for yourself and believe it to be true.

I live my life through a feminist lens—not because it's trendy—but because it's necessary. Because I've built something real in a world that wasn't built for women like me. Because I'm raising two daughters who will never shrink themselves to fit inside someone else's box.

I don't ask to be seen anymore. I show up and own it.

Now, when I walk into a room, I'm not performing. I'm remembering. I'm grounded in the energy of a woman who turned survival into power.

That's what Statement Peace has always been.

Not jewelry. Not a product. A frequency. A becoming. A reclamation.

I didn't follow a map. I followed my own compass. And it led me right back to myself.

Because this isn't a story about jewelry. It's about what happens when a woman stops waiting to be chosen—and chooses herself instead. It's what happens when you create from soul. When you stop apologizing. When you stop shrinking. When you stop outsourcing your worth and start living like the Universe is already conspiring in your favor—because it is.

I didn't just create Statement Peace. I *am* Statement Peace.

I've watched people from all walks of life find pieces of themselves through this story—whether they discovered it through my jewelry, through my words, or through simply watching my journey unfold.

I never set out to inspire anyone else—I just kept following the path that felt true. But now, I get to speak at conferences, gatherings, and workshops—sharing everything I've learned about authenticity, energy, vibration, and what it really means to create a life that's aligned with who you are.

I don't just sell products. I teach women to trust themselves again.

And every time I stand on a stage or sit across from someone who says, *"Your story changed something for me,"* I'm reminded that Statement Peace was never just about me.

It's about all of us.

About Jessy

Jessy Lee didn't come from comfort—rather, she was raised with grit. From a childhood that made her hyperaware, wildly intuitive, and fiercely resilient, she learned early how to move through rooms that didn't feel safe and how to hold vision in places where none existed. She wasn't raised to be loud, but she was born to be heard.

In 2017, with a baby on her hip and another on the way, Jessy founded Statement Peace. She had a vision that no one else could see, but she could feel the success behind it in every cell of her body. And she refused to let it go. Against all odds, she kept building—brick by brick—with nothing but intuition and perseverance. Her drive was relentless. Her belief, borderline stubborn. And that persistence became her power. What started at her kitchen table grew into a globally recognized lifestyle brand, now carried in thousands of stores. But the success she's most proud of is knowing her daughters watched her do it. They saw what it looks like to back yourself fully—and bet on a vision no one else can see.

Somewhere along the way, Jessy recognized a pattern: when she created, she felt joy. When she felt joy, she felt gratitude. And when she felt gratitude, everything shifted—clarity, momentum, abundance. That rhythm became her compass. It's how she operates. It's how she builds. Jessy held down her household like an anchor while building a globally recognized brand—manifesting the life she dreamed of by holding the vision, trusting the patterns that served her, and staying in alignment no matter what.

https://statementpeace.com/
Instagram: @statement_peace

Black Bow Gifts
Lady Alisha Martin

People always say things like "I just want a new life."

They dream out loud about fresh starts and second chances— new careers, new love, a new body, a new car. And I get it. I used to say those things too.

But here's the thing no one tells you: New lives don't come wrapped in satin ribbons and gold foil. They don't arrive in a Tiffany-blue box with champagne and confetti.

The real life-altering gifts, the ones that truly change you, usually come in packages you never wanted and never asked for.

Mine came wrapped in twisted metal and hospital sheets.

It was an ordinary day. A routine drive. Until it wasn't. The crash was violent, unforgiving, and final in its own cruel way. I broke my neck and my back. In the blink of an eye, everything I had worked for, everything I had built, shattered.

The doctors delivered the verdict with all the softness of a hammer: *You will never walk unassisted again. And the likelihood of successful pregnancies is minimal.*

And just like that, I was handed my first black bow gift.

I didn't see it as a gift at the time. How could I? I was trapped in a body that no longer moved how I told it to. I cried. I screamed. I refused to believe this was my life now. But every day, I woke up still broken and still breathing.

In that breath, I began to rebuild.

It wasn't fast. It wasn't pretty. Recovery rarely is. It took five long years of being bedridden or using wheelchairs and canes. Five years of learning how to live inside a body that had betrayed me. Five years of stripping down every identity I had ever held: boss, wife, woman, achiever. And in that rawness, I met someone new.

Me.

Not the me who had the perfect plan. Not the me who showed up strong and styled every day. But the me who knew pain and didn't run from it. The me who had lost almost everything and found herself anyway.

I started to call those moments *black bow gifts*.

Because that's what they are.

When people tell the universe, "I hate this life, I want a new one," they imagine winning the lottery or getting swept off their feet in Paris. But transformation doesn't work like that. Real change often shows up in the ugliest wrapping. Divorce. Bankruptcy. Betrayal. Loss. Accidents. Rock bottom.

The package is black and heavy, tied with a bow of grief. And yet, inside? Something sacred.

Inside my black bow gift, I found the most powerful parts of myself.

I found resilience I didn't know I had. I found purpose deeper than titles or paychecks. I found faith, not in miracles, but in movement. In tiny, trembling steps. In breath, in tears, in quiet.

Once my mind stopped asking *"why me?"* and started whispering *"what now?"* the shift began. Slowly, almost impossibly, my body started to follow my belief.

By the time I reached my thirteenth surgery, I had stopped waiting for someone to fix me and started advocating for myself. I chose to believe, out loud, that this wasn't a tragedy, it was a turning point. That mindset opened doors. Solutions I had never considered started showing up. By surgeries fifteen and sixteen, I was implanted with two neurostimulation devices, machines powered by internal batteries and threaded wires along my spinal cord. They delivered electrical pulses that disrupted the pain signals screaming at my brain. Technology met tenacity, and hope took root.

Against every prognosis and odd, I walked again.

That first step was more than medical; it was spiritual. Because I wasn't stepping into the old life I had lost. I was stepping into the new one I had earned.

I didn't go back to being the woman I was before the accident. I couldn't. That version of me didn't survive the crash. And honestly? Thank God.

The new me had no time for pretending or performing. I came back into the world sharper. Softer. Bolder. And absolutely unwilling to waste a single ounce of this second chance.

Professionally, I rose.

I didn't just get back into my work; I reimagined it. I became a leader, a voice, an advocate for the kind of change that doesn't just drive results, but drives people. I started shaping spaces where others could grow, be seen, be celebrated, not in spite of their struggles, but because of them.

I used every scar I carried as strategy.

I built programs that made people feel human again. I challenged systems that left folks behind. I advocated for women, for small businesses, for communities that needed more than charity; they needed opportunity. I wasn't just rebuilding my life; I was making room for others to do the same.

And just when I thought I had received the full extent of my transformation...

I got another black bow gift.

Just when I thought the hardest part was behind me, one of the machines failed. The pain returned. The fear returned. The surgery count started climbing again. For a moment, I felt betrayed all over, first by my body, now by the technology meant to save it. I told myself maybe I'd already used up all my miracles. Maybe I was asking for too much.

But life doesn't operate on timelines. It moves on truth.

And the truth was, I wasn't done.

Against every prognosis, every doubt, every internal whisper telling me not to hope, I had a baby in 2014.

I, the woman they said wouldn't walk again, gave birth, stood on my own two feet, and held new life in my arms. That child wasn't just a miracle. He was proof that joy can follow devastation. That hope grows best under all the scars.

I was present in a way I never could have been before. Every diaper, every giggle, every sleepless night, I soaked it in like someone who knew how easily it could've never been.

Now when people come to me and say, "I feel stuck. I want something new," I smile gently and ask:

"Are you ready to open a black bow gift?"

Because change, real change, isn't cute or chic. It doesn't come in rose gold. It shows up like a storm and asks who you are without the mask.

And if you let it? It will show you who you were meant to become.

I've come to believe that the worst things that ever happened *for* me weren't punishment. They were invitations. They were hand-delivered awakenings. And yes, they arrived messy. Devastating, even. But they carried exactly what I needed to grow, to shift, to slay.

So if you're reading this and your life feels like it's falling apart, if your heart is broken or your body is tired or your path just exploded into a thousand pieces, listen to me closely:

There's a gift in this.

It doesn't look like one. It doesn't feel like one. But I promise you it's in there.

Maybe it's a new strength. A new voice. A new mission. A new life.

But you won't find it until you unwrap it. Until you sit with the   mess. Until you dare to believe that beauty can be born in the dark.

Because it can. It does. It *has.*

My name is Lady Alisha Martin. I walked through fire, rolled through hell, and stood up anyway. I wear my black bows with pride.

They remind me that even when the wrapping looks like ruin, the gift inside can still be gold.

And that? That's how you slay.

About Alisha

Lady Alisha Martin, currently serves as the vice president of business development at Suncoast Credit Union, exemplifies leadership with a profound commitment to growth, sustainability, and the nurturing of strategic partnerships that resonate with the mission of Suncoast Credit Union. With over two decades of diverse experience in the financial sector, she brings a unique blend of expertise, passion, style, and resilience to her role, particularly distinguished by her personal mantra, "If I can get myself out of a wheelchair, I can do this. If you can get yourself out of bed, you can do this."

In her tenure at Suncoast Credit Union, Lady Alisha has been instrumental in sculpting the vision and operational strategy of the business development department. Her responsibilities encompass leading sales and development units, introducing innovative products and services, and spearheading campaigns that significantly enhance member engagement and retention.

A formidable advocate for economic inclusion and financial literacy, Lady Alisha is deeply involved in her community. She holds positions on various boards, including the Lakeland Chamber of Commerce and Leadership Lakeland Alumni. Her efforts extend into initiatives such as the Angel Foundation and the American Foundation for Suicide Prevention, underlining her dedication to societal welfare and economic development.

Lady Alisha is a celebrated public speaker and mentor, driven to educate and inspire individuals and businesses alike, fostering economic resilience and personal growth. Her academic credentials include a master of business administration, summa cum laude, from the University of Phoenix, and she continues to participate actively in professional development through several esteemed organizations that include Wharton, Stanford, and Yale School of Business.

Instagram: @thelishmartin
www.lishmartin.com

From Disconnection to Embodied Sovereignty

Valentina Mazzei

I was born in Rome, Italy, and raised in a loving but over-nurturing home that valued perfection, politeness, and approval above all else. From a young age, I absorbed a powerful—yet invisible—belief: that love must be earned, not lived. In my world, to be seen was to be good, to stay quiet, and to play nice. So I learned how to be the "good girl"—but not how to be myself. That conditioning followed me into adulthood and shaped my relationships.

My first love relationship, which spanned nearly a decade, was filled with adoration, but began before I truly knew who I was. As I grew, I outgrew him. After the breakup, a series of surface-level connections left me questioning my worth—until one volatile relationship cracked me open. During an argument that escalated into a panic attack in the car, I saw myself with sharp clarity: a woman gripping safety while abandoning my truth. That drive home became my tipping point. Months later, I took a bold leap and moved from Italy to Miami to follow the "American Dream." I built a polished corporate career, got married, and became a US citizen. From the outside, I had it all. But on the inside, I was still searching.

I thought marriage would complete me; instead, it mirrored back the parts of me I hadn't yet claimed. I didn't know how to fully see myself, so I sought wholeness in the reflection of another. My nervous system was bracing. My voice felt buried.

Then came the grief that cracked everything open: my mother-in-law was murdered by her husband's stepfather—a trauma that reopened old wounds and demanded deeper healing. It became a portal—not just into pain, but into truth. Both my husband and I had to break down in order to rebuild—

not into who we were before, but into who we came here to become.

Today, our relationship stands not as a rescue, but as a reunion of two people who chose to heal individually so they could rise together.

From that breaking came a breakthrough. I began to explore a new path rooted in ancient wisdom and spiritual technology. I immersed myself in sound healing, hypnosis, breathwork, plant medicine, and somatic embodiment.

In one powerful Ayahuasca ceremony, I didn't just experience frequency; I became it. Resonance moved from a concept to a body-based truth, like a river. My nervous system exhaled. My ego dissolved. I merged with Source. And for the first time, I felt myself beyond trauma. I remembered: I wasn't broken, just misaligned. Three years after first voicing my desire to co-facilitate sacred ceremonies, my shamans invited me to lead retreats beside them. It wasn't coincidence; it was confirmation. Proof that when energy aligns, manifestation becomes inevitable.

From there, I founded Where the Magic Happens, and began guiding sound bath meditations across Miami. The name wasn't just poetic; it was precise.

In the present moment, here and now—when the body is relaxed and the mind is awake—that's where and when the magic happens. That's where we become the creators of our lives, not the reactors. That's where nervous systems soften, timelines shift, and manifestations are no longer goals—but inevitabilities.

I soon left the corporate world, moved with my family to Naples, and birthed my signature frequency work: The Embodied Alchemy Code™—a multi-phase methodology designed to help high-achieving women drop survival responses and step into feminine power. My work bridges neuroscience and spirituality so women can manifest—not just with their minds, but with their bodies. I guide women through three alchemical phases—each one rooted in nervous system safety, energetic coherence, and soul-level manifestation.

Phase 1: The Reset - Shedding masculine overdrive and releasing survival-mode conditioning. This phase is about unwinding the hustle blueprint, healing shame and guilt around pleasure, and reawakening the body's intuitive voice. Through breath, sound, and somatics, women begin to remember: softness is strength.

Phase 2: The Rise - This is where the shift happens—from effort to embodiment. Women learn how to magnetize desires without force, anchor safety through sound, and reclaim their unapologetic voice. No more performing. Just presence.

Phase 3: The Return - Here, embodiment becomes identity. The feminine CEO is no longer performing leadership; she is the frequency of ease, radiance, and devotion. She holds her power without bracing. She leads from overflow. She remembers how to love without losing herself.

The full experience blends live sound activations, somatic rewiring, and frequency-based manifestation tools. It's not a course. It's a recalibration. And it works—because it meets women where they are... and anchors them into who they've always been.

Today, so many have returned to their radiance, reclaimed their voice, and remembered their sovereignty.

My next chapter is weaving this frequency lineage into a world-changing movement. As my *Brainz Magazine* interview affirms, I am committed to building a sanctuary of safety and transformation—a multi-sensory hub where energy aligns, consciousness expands, and feminine leadership is redefined.

My vision is to travel the world guiding transformational retreats that awaken, soften, and activate. To gather women in sacred spaces—on mountaintops, oceansides, and temples—where deep embodiment is no longer a concept but a lived experience. And ultimately, to build my own sanctuary: a permanent energetic vortex where healing, recalibration, and remembrance become a way of life.

This is about deepening presence.

I'm here to honor the frequency. To birth a lineage of embodied women who lead—not through force, but through resonance.

Selected for Slaying Naples, I'm not promising transformation.

I'm transmitting it. One breath. One sound. One woman at a time.

I was the little girl who performed. In school. In relationships. At home. I believed my value came from being helpful, perfect, productive. The more I achieved, the more I performed—and yet the emptier I felt.

Even after I moved to the United States, became a citizen, married, and built a corporate career, I was still chasing a version of myself that wasn't real. My nervous system was in survival mode. I looked successful. But inside, I was bracing, shrinking, disappearing. I felt unseen. Unworthy.

Truthfully, my real breakout hadn't happened when I moved; it had happened long before, in that invisible world of disconnection. The one where you feel like you should be someone else's version of "enough."

As a child, I often found myself in the trap of comparing, constantly seeking validation and acceptance while neglecting my own needs and desires. I felt the weight of others' expectations in my body: the people-pleasing that whispered "you are only loved when you're the good girl."

Marriage didn't free me—it mirrored my fractures, until I faced them and became whole without needing someone else to save me.

I didn't turn to spirituality out of desperation; I turned to it in rebellion—against the performance. I began with breathwork, plant medicine, energetic rituals. Then I found sound.

And in one ceremony, something clicked. I didn't hear frequencies—I became one. My brain dropped into Theta. My body softened into presence. And I felt it: the truth of who I was before the world told me to be anything else.

That moment didn't just heal me. It aligned me.

Three years after I first dreamed of leading ceremony, my shamans invited me to co-facilitate international retreats. The very thing I had imagined... manifested—without chasing, forcing, or controlling.

Shortly thereafter, I left corporate life. I created a path that mirrors what I lived through—The Embodied Alchemy Code™— a three-phase initiation that guides women from burnout into embodiment, from striving into softness, from performance into pure presence.

This isn't about becoming someone new. It's about remembering who already lives inside your cells.

I work with women who've consumed every course, every book, every strategy—and still feel empty. They stop performing and rise in sovereignty. They lead from pleasure, not panic. They soften—and become more powerful.

"Change your energy. Change your life." This isn't a mantra. It's a method.

Embodied certainty is different from performance-based belief. That was me—before full sovereignty.

But now I listen. I transmit. I remember. And so do they.

As a Brainz Magazine Executive Contributor, ISTA-certified sound practitioner, Mindvalley-trained facilitator, and devoted student of Dr. Joe Dispenza, I bring both structure and soul to this work.

What sets me apart is the lineage—from performance to presence. From child-healer to corporate woman to spiritual alchemist.

But the magic isn't in the method.

It's in the frequency.

I'm not here to teach empowerment.

I'm here to help women feel safe enough to embody it.

This isn't about ambition.

It's about anchoring into a new way of being.

My dream is to awaken the goddess in every woman—the goddess who's already there, hidden beneath approval, people-pleasing, and fear.

I don't just *believe* in your radiance; I see it. I see you.

If your body is softening... if your breath is slowing... if your heart is pounding—

That's not coincidence. That's resonance.

This is the work. This is the frequency. This is feminine leadership, redefined.

About Valentina

Valentina Mazzei is a sound alchemist and manifestation guide who bridges neuroscience and spirituality to catalyze deep cellular transformation.

Raised in Rome and reborn through rupture, Valentina spent years chasing perfection—until her body whispered the truth: she wasn't here to perform. She was here to remember.

Today, she helps high-performing women release survival-mode conditioning and rewire their nervous systems so they can soften, expand, and lead from embodied presence.

Through her signature framework, The Embodied Alchemy Code™, Valentina guides clients through a three-phase energetic recalibration—from burnout to softness, from performance to pure feminine power. Her work blends live sound activations, somatic rewiring, and frequency-based manifestation tools to create transformation at the root.

Valentina is an ISTA-certified sound practitioner, Brainz Magazine Executive Contributor, Mindvalley-trained facilitator, and a devoted Dr. Joe Dispenza student, who has studied under shamans, neuroscientists, and spiritual masters around the world.

Whether she's leading sacred retreats in Colombia, guiding meditations across South Florida, or helping women activate their goddess frequency online, her work is a transmission—not just a teaching.

Her mission: to awaken a lineage of embodied feminine leaders who no longer chase worth but remember it.

Instagram: @where.themagic.happens
Facebook: Where the Magic Happens Sound and Energy Alchemy
Website: www.wherethemagichappensnow.com (under construction)

Strength in the Struggle: My Unfiltered Story

Lori-Ann Marchese

My story didn't begin in the spotlight. It began in silence—in the quiet corners of classrooms where I was bullied from elementary through high school. I was called names like "ugly" and "buck-toothed beaver." Every word chipped away at my self-esteem. I became the girl who smiled on the outside but silently questioned her worth.

I'll never forget the friend who stood up for me when two girls wouldn't stop calling me ugly. His courage and kindness marked a turning point for me. Looking back, I now realize those years were shaping something deep within me—something stronger than I ever imagined.

In time, I found healing through health. I became a dental hygienist—not just because I cared about wellness, but because I wanted to help people smile confidently again. I knew the power of a smile—and the pain of hiding one.

But after graduating from hygiene school, I felt a deeper calling. I entered the world of fitness, and with it came new challenges—especially within my traditional Italian family. When I was competing in fitness shows, prepping meals instead of eating pasta on Sundays, even the scent of grilled chicken seasoned with Mrs. Dash became a problem. In our family, you ate what was made and sat at the table together.

They didn't understand the world I was stepping into or why I was so passionate about it. I wished they could see the "why" behind my sacrifices—why I gave so much to this journey. But I knew, even without their validation, I had to follow my path. I believed in something bigger. And one day, I hoped they would too.

I went on to earn titles like Miss Bikini New York America, Miss Fitness Model New York America, Miss Bikini New

England, Miss Summer Nationals, Miss Bikini Fitness Atlantic, and ultimately placed in the top three at the WBFF World Championship. These weren't just trophies—they were personal victories. Proof that I could rise above judgment, pressure, bullying, and tradition to follow my truth.

That journey brought incredible opportunities. I landed magazine covers, including two-time cover model for *Muscle & Fitness Hers*, and have been featured globally—including ongoing articles with *Bella Magazine*. But one of the most meaningful moments came when I competed for Mrs. Connecticut America—and my father was in the audience. When I won, he cried. After years of misunderstanding, that moment felt like a bridge back to belief.

My father had always understood me a little more—he was a taekwondo black belt competitor—so he got what it meant to train, sacrifice, and fight for a dream.

As my career grew, I founded Body Construct—an all-women's fitness facility where I could do more than help women change their bodies. I wanted to help them reclaim their confidence, shift their mindset, and find community. The gym became a second home for thousands of women, and seventeen years later, it still stands as a space of strength and sisterhood.

I've helped women lose five to one hundred pounds, both mentally and physically transforming their lives. Professionally, I've been recognized as one of the top fitness experts in the world by *Huffington Post New York*, appeared on Bravo's *Game of Crowns*, and coached thousands of women both in person and virtually.

But no title has ever meant more than being a mother—and being a woman who never gave up.

Behind the success, though, were silent battles. I cried in the car, during walks, in the bathtub, on my pillow at night. I often wondered, *Will there ever be a week without tears and a fake smile?*

During my marriage, I suffered the heartbreak of two pregnancy losses. But I kept showing up—smiling for clients, running my business, pushing through. Then came my miracle:

my daughter, Ariana. She became my why. My strength. My reason for every comeback.

Life seemed great. My business was thriving. My mom was a huge help with my daughter. But as time passed, I started noticing the shift—my mother and I were carrying the load while a distance grew in my marriage. After nearly eight years of trying to make it work, it became clear that we no longer shared the same vision or values. I was deeply hurt. Still, I stayed... until the pandemic hit.

Now I was facing the collapse of my marriage and a global shutdown. My business, my income—everything I had built—stood on shaky ground. But I didn't panic. I pivoted.

I launched Flat Belly On-the-Go, hand-packing smoothie meals with fruit, protein, and veggies. These weren't just nutrition—they were survival. Every cup sold kept my gym alive and reminded me and my clients that we were still standing.

But the struggle to stay open was still real, and we were still in the "red." I almost had to shut down one side of the gym. My only source of income was the smoothies I was hand-packing and selling. I'll never forget walking into the building for a meeting with my landlord, tears streaming down my face, and telling him I had to let go of one of my spaces. I felt defeated—but I had no choice.

He looked at me and said, "You've been dedicated here for over ten years. You always paid on time—if not early. I'm not going to let you shut it down."

Then he did something I'll never forget: he gave me two months of free rent to help me get back on my feet. I was overwhelmed with gratitude. He believed in me when I felt like I was losing everything.

He passed away in 2024, but his kindness and support will forever be in my heart.

Even through the struggle, I refused to give up on my ladies. This space was sacred. I poured my blood, sweat, and tears into keeping it alive—because I knew it wasn't just a gym. It was a lifeline.

The challenges kept rolling in! We were still going through the pandemic aftermath to rebuild what was lost. Eventually, I made one of the hardest—but bravest—decisions of my life: I got divorced. I never thought I would. The emptiness that followed was unbearable. I'd go out just to fill time. Weekends and holidays were the hardest—seeing couples and families everywhere while I was alone. I pushed through the pain, keeping busy with friends, business, and my daughter.

Today, my ex and I are committed to raising our daughter with love and respect—separately, but together in parenthood.

Eventually, I met a wonderful man. The first night we met, he told someone, "I'm going to marry this girl." We've had our share of ups and downs, as well as a break-up, but one thing I felt was a big connection in my heart. Our love is strong, and we understand that we need to work as a team to be successful in all aspects of life! He's a businessman who understands challenges, growth, and grit. He understands the importance of a relationship, raising children, and the challenges of a divorce. We have similarities that allow us to communicate and grow through the tough moments. He recognizes the passion I had for my gym and saw how much I'd endured. He even helped me give the gym a fresh look—restoring the spark I almost lost.

I've lost homes. I've lost relationships. I've rebuilt from scratch. But every time life tried to knock me down, I came back stronger. Because resilience lives in my blood. And purpose fuels my soul.

Today, I coach women nationwide in fitness, mindset, and self-worth. My message is not about perfection. It's about power—turning pain into purpose and loss into fuel.

So if you're reading this and your world feels heavy—know this:

You are not alone.

You are not broken.

And you are absolutely not done.

Your next chapter could be the one where you rise.

My life never fit a mold—and I'm proud of that.

This isn't the life I was raised to follow.

It's the life I was born to build.

About Lori-Ann

Lori-Ann Marchese is a globally recognized fitness expert, nutrition coach, and entrepreneur known for her powerful, results-driven approach to women's wellness through mind, body, and soul transformation. She is the founder and owner of Body Construct, an all-women's gym in Connecticut that has been empowering women for over fifteen years.

Lori-Ann offers virtual training programs and travels nationwide for exclusive personal training, bringing her signature coaching and energy to clients wherever they are. Her personalized approach, whether online or in-person, is designed to meet women exactly where they are and guide them toward lasting strength, health, and confidence.

Crowned Mrs. Connecticut America, Lori-Ann rose to national fame as a cast member on Bravo TV's *Game of Crowns* and continues to be a leading media personality. She has been featured on Great Day Connecticut (WFSB News) and in top media outlets, including ET!, *OK! Magazine, Star Magazine,* and *Muscle & Fitness Hers,* where she has also appeared on the cover. She was named one of the Top Trainers in the World by *Huffington Post New York.*

Lori-Ann is also a contributor to *Bella Magazine,* where she shares fitness, beauty, and mindset expertise. Through her media presence, gym community, and elite coaching, she continues to inspire women to become their strongest selves— inside and out.

www.BodyConstructFitness.com
Instagram: @bcgymct @loriann.marchese

The Mourning After: The Chrysalis Journey

Vickie Menendez

Where the soul breaks open, the blueprint for rebirth is revealed.

There's a moment, after the final breath, after the silence settles in like fog, when time stops moving the way it once did. You look around and realize the life you knew has unraveled. The pieces are still there, scattered like sacred debris, but they no longer make the same shape. That was me. I've lived that moment more times than I ever imagined possible.

People often ask how I survived the loss of four children, each one leaving in a different season, with a different lesson, under a different sky. They want to know how I kept breathing when it felt like my world had been hollowed out. But survival was never the question. I didn't want to just survive. I wanted to understand. And more than anything, I wanted to honor them in the way I lived after the dust had settled.

It wasn't the events themselves that defined me. It was what came after. The quiet. The aching. The going within. The reimagining of a life I never thought I'd be forced to reimagine.

In the aftermath, everything changed. My beliefs. My relationships. Even my body. Grief does that. It touches every layer of your being. Some people couldn't walk with me in this new chapter. That hurt. There was messiness. Confusion. Distance from people I once held close. But there was also something else. Something softer and harder to describe. A whisper. A knowing. A holy unfolding.

It didn't make sense at first. Not in the way the world asks things to make sense. But deep down, I began to see that this path had always been mine. What I once thought were random passions (my obsession with self-care, my love for healing rituals, my deep spiritual curiosity) were divine seeds planted long ago, waiting to bloom when I needed them most.

Every healing modality I'd studied, every breathwork session I'd taught, every journaling prompt or moon ritual or grounding practice I'd ever led became my lifelines. Not borrowed tools, but sacred instruments my soul had tucked away for safekeeping.

Writing *The Mother of All Memoirs* was part of that unfolding. It was a catharsis, yes. But more than that, it was a channel. A way for me to give voice to what had been buried in silence for too long. Each word I wrote was a breadcrumb back to myself. And as I wrote, I kept thinking... if even one woman reads this and sees her own possibility in my story, then my children's legacies are not just preserved, they're magnified.

I believe we make soul agreements before we ever arrive earthside. Contracts. Sacred pacts. And while I will never pretend to understand all the "whys," I do believe with every fiber of my being that we chose this. Me. My children. My father. We agreed to walk this path together, knowing it would require unthinkable surrender but also knowing the ripple it would create.

I no longer walk alone. I walk alongside my children, my dad, and every scar and sacred scarlet thread that binds me to this purpose. I walk in full acceptance that while the journey is messy, it is also miraculous. This is, to me, the essence of learning to live again.

I no longer see death as the end. I see it as a threshold. A veil. An exquisite, sacred passage. I stood at that threshold so many times, and each time I came back changed. Awakened. Split open and filled with something greater than logic can explain. My children didn't leave me. They simply stepped into a different role in our contract. They are closer now than ever, guiding, whispering, moving through me in ways I could never have imagined.

There is a beauty to death that I never saw before. A tenderness. A holiness. And I get to carry that now, not just for myself, but for the women who are still navigating their own dark nights.

The last two years have been the most illuminating of my life. Not because they were easy. But because I finally stopped trying to outrun the pain and started listening to what my body, my soul, and my Creator were trying to tell me. Our bodies speak in whispers. And if we don't listen, they find other ways to be heard louder, deeper, and through the very symptoms we often try to ignore. I let my own self-care wisdom, built over decades, become my compass. I let grace lead. And in doing so, I stepped into the kind of service that I know my children would be proud of.

Each of my losses brought a different level of awakening.

The first cracked me open with questions. Why me? Why this? That experience is what led me to begin looking at life through a more spiritual lens.

The second nudged me toward healing, though I didn't yet know what that would look like. I also realized later that this nudge was what prepared me for the most profound loss.

The third and fourth, those sacred, searing losses that came just twelve days apart, lifted me to a higher vantage point. One I almost don't have words for. One I sometimes can't believe I was given.

But something else began to rise, too.

With each loss, old wounds I thought I had buried began asking for my attention. The grief of the present was undeniable, but it came hand in hand with the grief of the past. It was as if everything I had survived silently was suddenly demanding to be seen.

I began to remember the dysfunctional home I grew up in. The volatility. The confusion. And yet, somehow, in that chaos, my father's soul found a way to offer us a lifeline. He taught us how to sing. It wasn't just music. It was a spiritual vibration, a frequency that surrounded my tender heart with something that felt safe.

I think back to the day my dad and I were building a rock wall together. Just the two of us, stacking stones in silence until he paused and looked at me. He said, "Vickie, I think you could do anything you set your mind to." He didn't say things like that often. That sentence became a stone in my foundation. It still holds me up when everything else feels like it's falling apart. I chose to focus on the moments that supported and empowered me. Those became my lifelines.

But even that foundation was shaken when another layer surfaced: the trauma I hadn't spoken aloud until I was sixty years old. The truth of my sexual trauma, held in silence for decades. It rose up after the overdose of my son. That moment brought to light everything I had been holding beneath the surface.

These were not isolated events. Each grief pulled up the root systems of every pain that had gone unhealed. Because that's what grief does. It doesn't just take you to the edge of what's happening now. It takes you to everything that has ever lived in your shadow.

But here's the miracle: we get to choose what we do with it. We can fall under the weight of it, or we can meet it with compassion, presence, and a willingness to become. No matter what happens in our lives, we can see the gifts revealed through these experiences if we choose to.

But I know who spoke those truths into my life.

It was something greater. God, Spirit, Source—whatever name you give the sacred presence that whispers beyond the veil. It came gently but clearly, through signs, through silence, through the undeniable thread of meaning that wove itself through every unbearable moment.

"I am not what happened to me. I am what I choose to become."
— Carl Jung

This is not a chapter about despair. It's a chapter about returning to life. A life reimagined. Rebuilt from ashes, yes, but infused with a brilliance I could never have accessed without the fire.

I no longer walk alone. I walk with grace, with grief, with reverence. I walk with the certainty that every breath I take carries the essence of those I've lost and the wisdom I've earned.

And if you're reading this, I want you to know something.

Your life, too, holds that same thread of beauty. Even if right now all you see is dust.

When you're ready, when the fog begins to lift, you'll see it. The light. The possibility. The hand on your shoulder that says, "You were never alone."

It's why I created *Compass to the Soul: Your Healing Companion,* a sacred guide for those ready to move beyond the aftermath and into the healing that awaits on the other side of loss.

Because what happened to me wasn't just loss.

It was a divine preparation.

A soul remembered.

A woman reimagined.

About Vickie

Vickie is a lifelong seeker, guide, and sacred space holder devoted to helping women rise from the ashes of grief and trauma to enter the sacred unfolding of their becoming. With over thirty-five years in the field of wellness and self-care, her journey has been deeply shaped by the profound personal loss of four children and her father. Each of them continues to walk beside her in spirit. Rather than letting her pain define her, Vickie transformed it into purpose. She has birthed a body of work that honors healing, ritual, and the soul's sacred agreements.

She is the author of *The Mother of All Memoirs—Crystal's Butterfly Effect* and the creator of Learning to Live Again, a movement and mentorship space for those navigating the complexities of life after loss. Her offerings now include *Compass to the Soul: Your Healing Companion* and *The Chrysalis Code*: sacred resources designed for those ready to move beyond the aftermath and into a healing journey that gently holds space for them to blossom into their true essence.

Through guided workshops, writing, breathwork, and intimate storytelling, she invites others into the gentle, courageous act of reimagining their lives. Vickie believes we are never alone, even in our deepest grief. What remains and rises is our true essence.

This Is What It Means to Be Home: A Story of Love, Faith, and Real Estate

Kimberley Menkhorst

I can pinpoint the exact moment everything changed for me, pushing me forward on a trajectory I never planned or saw coming. It was one decision: moving to Naples, Fla.

This single decision catapulted a journey like a game of dominoes falling into place. To understand how I got here, it's important to understand where I began.

I grew up in a small town in South Central Pennsylvania. I had an idyllic childhood filled with love, family, and a strong work ethic. The lessons my parents taught me as a child were guided by faith. They taught me early how to treat others with kindness, and how to put my all into everything I did, whether the job was big or small. I still live by these principles today. Since I was a small child, I always knew that, no matter what happened in life, I could come home to a safe place. That feeling gave me the courage to go out and explore the world, confident I had nothing to lose. That international travel experience was a turning point, fostering my independence from a young age.

When the time came to go to college, I chose a warmer climate and majored in advertising, which landed me at a small private school in North Carolina. I graduated a semester early and wasn't sure where I wanted to go. I knew I didn't want to stay there, yet I wasn't ready to go home. I wanted to see what else the world had to offer. I ended up working as a marketing coordinator for an architect in Miami. I enjoyed the job but hated living in Miami. So after two and a half years, an opportunity arose to work in Naples for the largest privately held commercial construction company in Florida as their marketing director.

Previous to this, I had only been to Naples once for a conference and only left the hotel for one dinner. I knew nothing about Naples other than it was a retirement city (I was twenty-four). I got the job and decided on a whim to move. I figured if I hated it I could spend a few years and move again. I moved here not knowing one person within hundreds of miles. I had ZERO idea that it would be the best decision I ever made.

Just three months after I moved, my new boss set me up on a blind date with his cousin. That cousin is now my husband, and we've been together over eighteen years. He had just moved from the Netherlands, and we hit it off from day one.

Sounds great, right?

But about three months later, just as things felt like they were falling into place, I got the most shocking news: a cancer diagnosis out of the blue. I was a healthy twenty-four-year-old who worked out six times a week, was eating healthy, and had barely even had a cold in the past year. The diagnosis: Non-Hodgkin's Lymphoma.

When you get that kind of news, you don't know what to expect, because all you ever hear are the negative stories associated with cancer. You feel it's a death sentence. I didn't know if I would make it to thirty, let alone live a long life. Fear can grip you, but I relied on faith to heal me. I told you I grew up with unwavering faith in God—but I had no idea this journey with cancer would be my biggest test of faith.

I had just started dating my husband... I wondered, *Now what?* We were having a great time, but we barely knew each other. I was going to be bald, and I thought, *Who would want to date a girl with cancer that they'd just met*?

My boyfriend had taken care of me after surgery to remove the lymph node, and he took off work to go to the doctor's office with me to hear the news that it was cancer. He gave me a nervous speech outside the doctor's office about how we were going to get through this, and said all the right things. He told me later he cried the entire way back to work, calling his aunt to listen. A guy with a big heart, a sweet soul... but in reality, he barely knew me.

The entire time, he never wavered. He shaved my head, sat with me when I was so tired I couldn't get off the couch, and he made life *fun*. He and his cousin would take me to dinner and take me to do fun things. Their goal was to keep me smiling and just living life through it all. A series of miracles that could be an entire book on its own began to happen, and I saw the silver lining in the entire journey along the way. God blessed me through it all.

I grew at work, got promoted, and *loved* the people and the work. We were winning every job, and we built most of the buildings, schools, condos, and skyline of Naples. It was fun and creative, and I learned so many skills. During that time, I personally helped secure over $1.2 billion in jobs throughout Florida, and then our company got bought out.

The doctor told me I probably wouldn't have kids after treatment. In the hardest decision I've ever had to make, I chose to trust God completely and not freeze my eggs. I stood on my faith and believed God would know the desires of my heart and bless me with a miracle baby one day.

A few years later, we got married and wanted to try for kids right away. I quickly got pregnant with our first baby with zero issues.

After her birth, I began to crave having my own business, but had no idea what that would look like.

Everyone told me to get into real estate, but I was shy and introverted, preferring to be behind a computer. By chance, I met a successful luxury agent who convinced me to work part-time for him. I handled all his marketing, and he saw I thought completely different about things, so he asked me to restructure his business. I enjoyed the work and the fast-paced world, but I also saw how crazy these agents got, how stressful it could be, and I said more times than I could count that I would *never* be a real estate agent.

But God had other plans.

When I decided to get into real estate, I'd just had my second baby, and I had *zero* idea where to start in this oversaturated market. I knew I could market things really well, but I was introverted and hardly knew anyone. How was I going to find clients? My husband and others saw in me what I didn't see in myself. It was that love and support my husband gave me that has everything to do with the success I've had.

The first eight months started slowly, with many ups and downs, as any business owner can understand. But I was determined to give it my all and make it work. By January the following year, I had over twenty million dollars in listings and a growing pipeline. For the first few years, I HUSTLED. I worked seven days a week, all hours of the day, met people, created resources, and built a business from scratch. When I started seeing consistent business year after year, I realized I had the success in numbers and money, but not in time and freedom like I craved. I wanted to run a business, not have the business run me.

The best thing to happen to my business was 2020. I took a deep breath, stepped back, and got laser-focused on attracting the clients I *wanted* to work with. I set boundaries, and clients respected them. I created so much content and resources for my customers, and started a YouTube Series about Naples, Fla. (Check it out and subscribe @LivinginNaplesFL) I dove into providing more value to my customers while working fewer hours, *and* I made more money!

In the last few years, I've realized I want more of this kind of balance. I want to give customers the best experience buying or selling–and I also want my kids and family to feel I'm fully present and not always thinking about work.

I kept searching for an answer for how to find an even better balance but couldn't find what I was looking for. Again, in God's perfect timing, I met a lady in 2024 at a mastermind who is now my business partner, and we created a platform to not only solve my problems but to help other agents.

Our "Fill in the Gaps" real estate platform is for other agents who struggle with work-life balance, always feel like they're behind and not doing enough, or are just burnt out and don't have time for one more thing. This system gives back so much time while taking away the stress. It's the missing piece for solo agents to scale.

The program puts every system in one place. It includes AI automation from leads and nurture to modern branded marketing materials. The content is not just generic real estate fluff we're all sick of reading. This is *relevant* content *niched* to the agent's target audience.

The platform features a CRM with details to create an amazing customer experience for referrals, *and* incorporates all the marketing campaigns to market homes (emails, timelines, eight-page magazine brochures, etc.). You can order and print anywhere in the country from the program, with a site for adorable merch, closing gifts, yard signs, and all the fun stuff for open houses. It's the all-in-one marketing, administration, and operational system that agents have been missing.

In addition, there is true community around this product; we are connecting visionaries around the country, not only for referrals but for real growth, masterminding in a safe space, and brainstorming ideas and issues without fear of a local agent trying to duplicate them.

I feel I have fully come into alignment with God's plans for my life. I truly wake up daily with so much gratitude for life, for health, for my two healthy kids, and an amazing husband who loves me unconditionally. If it wasn't for a husband who fully supported my dreams and ambition (plus all my crazy ideas and home remodeling projects), I would NOT be where I am today. He's my partner in everything, and words could never describe my feelings for him.

I'm excited for the future—to help others buy and sell in, around, and out of Naples, Fla. And to help other agents remove the busy work and stress of marketing and operations, while they focus on their clients and family time, without sacrificing money.

I feel I have been blessed to be a blessing to others.

Sometimes I think about that scared twenty-four-year-old, wondering what her life would look like... if she would not only survive but thrive. I wish I could go back to her worried mind, give her a hug, and assure her that life is going to far exceed her expectations.

About Kimberley

Meet Kimberley Menkhorst, who moved to Naples in 2007, met her husband on a blind date three months later, and was diagnosed with cancer shortly after. Now thriving, she runs a successful real estate business, hosts the YouTube series "Living Lavish in Naples," and is expanding nationwide with a tech platform designed to help agents scale their business through automation.

Instagram: @lavishlivingsnaplesfl
YouTube: @LivinginNaplesFl

Diamond Strong: My American Dream

Diamond Darling

After taking care of my very sick mother, I needed a break. After the battle that we won—my mother's health improved and she was independent again—I chose to chase my dreams. My younger sister and I took a leap of faith: we wanted to go from Poland to America, specifically to visit New York City.

My American dream was a lottery on thin ice.

We sweated it out in the US embassy in Krakow, praying we would get our tourist visas. The waiting game was misery, but then ... we were going to America! On July 22, 2004, we dove into the unknown. As we arrived in New York City, number one on my bucket list, I was excited. The thrill of the unknown was intoxicating—visiting a new continent sounded like science fiction. My heart danced with excitement and fear.

Celebrating my twenty-first birthday in the city that never sleeps was a surreal experience, a dream within a dream. I was young and full of hope. What did I know about life? Two months of adventure was all I had planned, but life had other ideas, just like in a casino when you play poker and you GO ALL IN. I decided I need to come up with a reason to stay in the United States. The Big Apple vibes, straight from the movies, made me long for more. I had always dreamed of experiencing the city's magic firsthand, and being there was like a dream come true.

I decided to chase my dreams and give New York City a chance to show me everything it could. I had to see if I could make it in my dream city.

My sister, on the other hand, returned home, finished college, and achieved her degree. I'm beyond proud of her.

As a small town girl from Poland, I was amazed by Manhattan. Huge skyscrapers, the heartbeat of the traffic, and millions of people from all walks of life. Every minute was a "wow" moment, a reminder that the world was full of endless possibilities.

One day, I walked down 5th Avenue, feeling out of place. The fancy stores with fancy windows seemed like a world away. Everything felt just out of reach. At that moment, I would never in a million years have thought that in 2019 I would have a designer shoe closet with a huge collection that would be featured on national TV by Fox5 and Telemundo. With a pocket full of hope and only four hundred thirty dollars to my name, my dreams began to unfold that day, though.

I was in the middle of agonizing weeks of financial desperation that felt like an eternity. I almost lost my hope, and I was considering going back to Poland. I was lost, tears streaming down my face, but then I met someone. Although I was disappointed that I wasn't able to build the life I had hoped for, falling in love changed my heart. I wanted to stay and see what the next chapter held.

We got married a short time later, and it led to a practical solution for my future. With my papers in order, I could finally move forward with confidence. I felt like I finally had wind under my wings. Remembering that I was captivated by Audrey Hepburn in *Breakfast at Tiffany's* in the scene in the diamond district, I took my first solo subway trip to 47th Street. At the time, I couldn't afford the diamonds that sparkled in the sunlight in the window displays, but I knew at that moment I found my "forever love."

I set the goal—I wanted to work in the jewelry industry. I talked to my then husband about his connections, and he helped me schedule my first job interview at a diamond exchange in Bowery. From that moment on, I believed that everything happens for a reason, and life's unexpected twists bring people and experiences our way for a purpose. I believe that there are no coincidences in life.

I went for that interview. I was so unsure, totally green and clueless about jewelry and diamonds—I just knew I loved them. And I landed the job! It was as if the universe smiled upon me and made it happen.

I manifested that with all my heart! Prayed so much. On September 22nd, I took my first step into the unknown; my spirit was determined. I promised myself that I would learn with every passing day. I found out about the Gemological Institute of America (GIA) school, but that was a dream, out of my financial reach then, yet I refused to let that stop me.

Janet was the store owner, a shining light and hope in my life at that time. She saw potential in me and gave me a chance to grow, teaching me the ins and outs of the business. Her faith in me changed everything, and her impact played a big role in my decision to stay and climb the career ladder. Thank you Janet, I'll be forever grateful.

I chose to focus on the huge opportunity that lay before me. I was over the moon. It was time for me to work. The Christmas season was very busy with sales, with weeks of nonstop hassle. The line was twice as long as the counter, filled with clients trading their hard earned dollars for sparkles. I was crushing it, saving every penny for a car. That season was great, so I decided to shop for a car despite not having a driver's license yet.

I always wanted a Mercedes, but my husband set up an appointment in a different dealership, one I didn't want to go to. As I waited at the desk in the dealership, I noticed the messy papers and the salesman's metal name tag. I thought, *What an interesting last name...* I even said it in my head, together with my first name. Little did I know, it would soon become mine.

As for love at first sight ... I wasn't sold on a car but on the man behind the name. Talk about an awkward situation! How could I explain to my husband that I fell in love at first sight with the salesperson?

The end of our marriage had been a long time coming anyway, and the paperwork soon followed. Ironically, finishing that marriage took far longer than the marriage itself.

Then the dealership called because my car needed service. We reconnected. First drink. First dinner. First kiss. A beautiful tale of love and growth: we danced through two amazing years of dating, exploring breathtaking destinations together. During that time, in 2008, I achieved my long-time dream by graduating from GIA.

We got married in 2011, and soon after, our precious son brought new joy to us. Our little family blossomed.

I nestled into a cozy life at home, taking a break from the diamond industry to care for our family. Then, in 2018, my world crashed down when I suffered a life-altering ischemic stroke, but I beat the odds and recovered. I'm grateful for a second chance at life.

After almost twelve years of marriage, we parted ways in 2021. Like seasons change, sometimes, love stories take a turn. Heartbreak swept in, leaving me lost and vulnerable, unseen and unheard. It hurt so much when our marriage ended.

Months after, I fell into a new relationship that didn't work out, but it brought me and my son to Naples, Fla.

With hope in my heart, I searched for a new beginning in Naples. I was looking for a job I loved. For two years, I worked for two reputable jewelers, continuing my passion.

My Naples became my little slice of heaven. It was a different path from what I had planned, but it led to a brighter future.

After the heartache, I refocused on what truly matters—my fourteen-year-old son, my top priority. That's when "Diamond Darling World" came into the spotlight—the culmination of nineteen years of chasing more than a nine to five.

I created something luxurious, something that ignited joy. My passion for what I do makes me happy.

Jewelry holds a special place in my heart—it's a symbol of life's special moments, strong emotions, milestones, and big love. Passed down through generations, it tells a story of its own. I love bringing luxury to my clients' doorsteps. I'm all about personalized service, top-notch quality, and competitive pricing.

I'm honored to be a part of this luxurious world, and I put my heart into every piece while I'm designing, doing what I love with passion.

My story is a testament to the power of following your dream. And I am humbled to be a part of this book. Giving back is in my DNA. I am all about supporting amazing charities. I have walked in shoes that are too tight, too worn out, and too hard to fill. But those tough days taught me the value of compassion, empathy, and love.

I'm grateful for the amazing people who've crossed my path. Their kindness and support have been crucial in getting me to where I am today.

Diamonds shine with beauty—no headache, only sparkle and delight.

I believe that everything, good or bad, is a lesson, and as long as I learn from it, I move forward. For me, the only thing that truly matters is the present moment—not the shadows of yesterday or the unknown of tomorrow. Since the past is beyond my control, I focus on what I can do now—in the present, this valuable moment.

I am grateful for my twenty-one year's journey in America, no grudges no regrets. To be continued...

About Magdalena

With hope and dreams in her heart, Diamond Darling followed her soul to America. As she navigated the ups and downs of life, she discovered her passion for diamonds and jewelry, and worked tirelessly to build a career that brings joy and luxury to others.

She learned to appreciate the beauty of the present moment and is grateful for a second chance at life after a life-altering experience. As the founder of Diamond Darling World, Magdalena is dedicated to sharing her love of jewelry and sparkle with others, one beautiful piece at a time. She is reminded of the power of following her dreams.

Anything is possible.

@DiamondDarlingWorld
www.DaimondDarlingWorld.com

Building My Own Legacy
Elizabeth Pezzello

My journey has always been about bold pivots, personal growth, and following my passions.

I began my athletic career at age seven when I swam competitively on my local summer team. Throughout my childhood I exceled in athletics, including swimming and martial arts. It recently became clear to me how both of these sports would forever shape my future.

While athletics were my forte and focus throughout middle school and high school (I also swam for two years at the College of Mount Saint Vincent), my academics always fell a bit short. I struggled during my junior and senior years of high school and actually attended an alternative senior year program called Walkabout in Yorktown Heights, NY. This program was very much about selecting students with talent who didn't fit into the standard public-school setting. We participated in internships and community service, and instead of gym class, we had two weeks of backpacking in the Catskill and Adirondack mountains.

I guess you could say my journey continued to be nontraditional as I attended three different undergraduate colleges before earning my bachelor's degree from SUNY (State University of New York) Purchase (Stanley Tucci's alma mater) in 2013, which was two years later than it "should" have been. A switch in me flipped during my senior year at SUNY Purchase when I was enrolled in art classes and film classes and earned my proudest A+ on my seventeen-page senior capstone paper, where I wrote about Harvey Milk. My obsession with being grammatically correct also kick-started here as my professor was an excellent linguist.

One thing I remember most about my college journey was admiring my female professors. There was something so fascinating about being an expert in the field and being organized and educated enough to teach at a college.

My first real job was at a screen-printing company called Saati. I was the youngest person at work, and I was very proud to hold a well-paying job with benefits, 401k, the whole nine yards. I was thankful for the opportunity to run my own sales territory and make many connections that I still have to this day, which spoke to my entrepreneurial spirit. While I enjoyed a couple of years in this role, I learned quickly that sitting at a desk was certainly not what I wanted to do.

After ending my time at Saati, I began working as house manager for two different families in Westchester, NY. I enjoyed the mix of tasks and variations day-to-day, as well as being an integral part of someone's family. It was very satisfying. Again, something about multitasking and having no two days look similar kept my mind challenged and fulfilled.

A lot of my life has been about overcoming imposter syndrome. I told myself I needed to do things a certain way to fit in, but none of them ever rang true to me. From an outside perspective, I continued to excel and shape my life into what it is today, but as many of us know, it certainly never feels that way in the moment. Constant pivots can feel like starting over again, and while it doesn't delete or take away from previous progress, it sure does feel like it in the moment.

There is so much to learn from trial and error. As I continued on my educational journey, I began taking prerequisite courses for speech pathology at Lehman College in the Bronx. I absolutely loved being on campus, and I had finally reached an age where I could appreciate the opportunity to embrace higher education. I would drive to campus three nights a week after work and thoroughly enjoyed sitting in the front of the classroom, answering questions, and participating in extracurricular activities at school. I even had the opportunity to work on a project with Mark Messier, former professional hockey player.

Today I hold two master's degrees from the University of Bridgeport in business administration, as well as human nutrition. I fought hard for both of these degrees, earning my MBA while working for Dropbox in San Francisco, and finishing my degree in human nutrition days after giving birth to my daughter in 2022. I have a photo of myself finishing my final research paper for my second master's degree while Frankie slept next to me; she was about two days old.

Often throughout the years, I would pause to ask myself what direction I wanted to go in, struggling to pinpoint what I wanted to be when I grew up (haha). My commitment to athletics and nutrition was always a part of my identity. Even after ending my college swimming career, I swam competitively in San Francisco on a masters team, ran a half marathon, competed in multiple Ragnar relay races and Warrior Dashes, and attended workout classes whenever I could. One of my favorite stories to tell is while I was on a family vacation in Sweden in 2019, I walked over a mile in a snowstorm to attend a Barry's Bootcamp class. I bought a Lululemon zip up that says "Barry's Stockholm" on it that I will never get rid of!

My journey continued across various industries, and I wound up opening The Vitamin Bar in March of 2021 in Naples, Fla. This was my first business and a brand new industry for me. With no medical background, I quickly learned a lot about IV placement, nursing, and patient care as it pertained to our clients. I completed a certificate in IV therapy, as well as phlebotomy, that would allow me to be more hands on in the business, which is truly insane given the fact that I almost fainted when I got my first IV treatment. This business jives well with my passion and education in nutrition, and I currently offer nutrition coaching through my other business, Happy Health.

Nothing could have prepared me for coming across my true passion, though, which is bodybuilding. After hiring a coach in 2023, less than a year after having a baby, I set out on my bodybuilding journey. As an avid gym goer and competitive athlete by nature, the combination of hitting the gym while working toward a goal lit a fire in my soul. After spending several months building muscle through a strict meal plan and structured gym sessions, I began the preparation for my first bikini bodybuilding shows in 2024. I spent twenty-two weeks on a strict meal plan—no eating out, no alcohol, no sugar, and no processed foods—as well as a rigorous cardio protocol that was between thirty to sixty minutes, seven days a week. I shocked myself by placing very well at two shows in Florida: the Tampa Pro and the Mel Chancey Harbor Classic. My love for bodybuilding was born, and I absolutely love to share my knowledge with my clients and friends, as I understand how fascinating and curious the bodybuilding world is.

The biggest takeaway for me from competitive bodybuilding has been the explosive mental growth. There is something that happens when you go through an exhausting, rigorous preparation, to step on stage leaner than you've ever been in your life, only to be judged by a panel who is looking for any flaws in your physique. For me, the physique I built was just the cherry on top of a whole new woman who emerged from this process.

Today, I am honored to be working on the datacenter operations team at Google. Each and every path I chose to take throughout my life has led to this point. I am in a position where I can utilize my creativity and unique background to change people's experiences at Google and make a lasting impact. My plan is also to work on a nutrition and fitness program to be rolled out to Google datacenters, and hopefully one day Google wide.

My journey has been built on setting goals, achieving them, and continuing the journey. I aspire for so much and I am proud of the legacy I am building for myself, as a role model to my daughter and to all women who have the passion to do what they love and make a difference.

About Elizabeth

Elizabeth Pezzello is a powerhouse mom, wellness advocate, and tech professional who has mastered the art of reinvention. After owning and operating the Vitamin Bar, she recently took on a new role at Google while continuing to inspire others through fitness competitions and holistic health. Her story is one of bold pivots, empowered choices, and showing her daughter what's possible when you bet on yourself.

Elizabeth was born and raised in Mount Kisco, NY, and has lived in various places throughout the country, including San Francisco, Calif; Park City, Utah; Naples, Fla.; and now Nashville, Tenn. Each career opportunity forced her out of her comfort zone and showed the opportunity for passions to connect no matter what her job title was. Elizabeth holds two master's degrees from the University of Bridgeport in business administration, as well as human nutrition. No matter where she goes, peers look to her for health and wellness advice as she consistently displays what a healthy lifestyle looks like. While juggling being a mother to her beautiful daughter, Francesca, Elizabeth is still able to prioritize her goal of becoming a professional bodybuilder. Constantly learning and winning through both losses and successes, Elizabeth hopes to spread the message that no dream is too big, and you CAN have it all if you are willing to commit to your goals and make sacrifices for your success.

@theelizabethgorman
@thevitaminbarnaples

Brighter than Blonde
Christina Payton

"We're doing this."

It was February 2015. When I left the frigid temperatures and my career as a hairstylist in the Chicago suburbs for the tropical dreams of Naples, I never could have imagined what would come next. All I knew for certain was I was tired of being cold and was craving a challenging new career adventure.

After the cross-country move and a few months working at a local Naples salon, I realized I was still searching for a salon setting that captured my Midwest work ethic and the elevated guest experience I had come to value. Since I couldn't find what I really desired, I decided to create it and started with my own suite. I went straight to a place that excited me, downtown 5th Avenue. I found a second-story suite with a view of palm tree-lined sidewalks and luxury boutiques, signed a lease, and headed downstairs to a restaurant with my laptop in hand. I registered a business name, created a business card, and toasted to new beginnings.

I spent the next few weeks designing and building out my new salon home. On a quiet morning in June, I turned the key to the door and walked into my tiny, one-station salon suite, heart pounding louder than a hair dryer. That day, I was not just a stylist trying to stand out; I was a woman about to dive all-in, with no safety net. It felt like the stage of a one-woman show. It was my turning point.

Having previously thrived in high-volume, upscale salons, I had always been a part of a team and had a sense of community, and there had always been someone to figure out all the operational elements. My career as a Certified Redken colorist and Redken Artist had been built on copious amounts of education, creating great hair, and making guests feel their best. I took those strengths and created a foundation for my solo quest. I knew I could figure out the operational pieces in time.

Time flew quicker than I anticipated, and through networking, my dedication to social media, and referrals, my single-chair suite was attracting more than it could handle. While fulfilling, the long days and late nights there started to become lonely. As I continued to keep up with demand, I started to wonder what was next. *How long could I sustain the intense pace I was working? Should I start to look for an assistant?* Little did I know, I was manifesting that my one-woman suite was about to grow.

Soon, other stylists who had been watching my journey on social media began to inquire in-person how to join my "team." Over the next few years, my team organically began to form. Walls expanded to join more suites together. After the fifth suite was added, a new dream was starting to develop. I remember standing there knowing I had to make a decision if the next step, having my own brick and mortar salon with my name on a building, was my fate. Unsure, yet fiercely determined, it hit me. It was now or never. I went home that night and stared into the mirror. The woman staring back looked tired, uncertain, yet electrified. I whispered to her, "We're doing this."

That leap, leaving behind relying only on myself for the possibility of growing others, shaped the essence of who I became: the woman who built House of Blondes® by Christina Payton, a salon that's not just about hair, but about celebration. Today, with a team of talented stylists from around the world and support staff that elevates each guest's experience, the 2,000-square-foot space in downtown Naples shines brightly in so many ways that light up my heart. With its sparkling chandeliers, industrial glam design, and signature Blonde Bar, the salon stands as proof that daring begins with a single step forward.

Roots in Risk and in Heart

The early days of moving to the new space were chaotic: moving supplies, training on new color lines, converting to digital scale systems, recruiting a support staff, press releases, juggling guests and so much more. Every day and every late night, in addition to being behind the chair, I worked with business coaches on operations and trained and cheerleaded the team, trying to absorb this new world of owning a large salon. I had goals to build a salon where stylists and guests alike thrived. While the challenge to push myself to grow as a woman, business owner, and leader was sometimes greater than I thought I could handle, I knew the impact my hard work would have on so many. If I was going to do this, I was going to *do* this.

But the real transformation came with each person who walked in for a confidence boost, a conversation. Our team would listen to their stories and fears, learning about their after-school routines, or upcoming weddings. In return, we handed them a mirror moment where they could see their best selves. That emotional exchange, that trust, was the invisible thread I wove through House of Blondes. Three years after first opening our new location, I still pinch myself when I pass by our front windows and see glowing faces, wild laughter, and freshly styled strands bouncing under chandelier light.

Where Artistry Meets Integrity

Crafting beautiful hair is one thing. I set out to go beyond and create a hair wellness journey alongside beautiful hair goals. I wanted to change the game of highlighting hair and raise the expectations of our guests. I had come to realize that including services that preserved the hair's integrity in highlighting services was not an option, it was necessary. It's why we pioneered our *4P Hair Wellness* approach: *Prepare, Prevent, Protect, Prolong.* We don't just paint color and lightener. We consider scalp health, strand integrity, and most certainly long-term care. We ensure guests leave feeling secure in both look and longevity.

And amid all this technicality, our personal heart remains. Guests don't just come for a new shade, they come for the energy, the community, the champagne-fueled conversations at the Blonde Bar, the excitement when they first flip their hair. That atmosphere isn't by accident; it's by intention, by remembering that every client is more than a service ticket.

They're a story, a sister, a bride, a blank canvas maybe too haunted by old doubts. My hope is that they leave believing, even a little, that transformation isn't just outer—it's deeply internal.

Centering Community, Not Just Guests

Building House of Blondes wasn't only about having gorgeous hair; it was about having a community. I wanted a space where stylists could grow into artisans and humans grow into extensions of passion, support, and creativity. We've curated a dream team of color specialists, extension artists, and guest-service experts, all aligned to elevate others the way I once needed to be elevated.

One evening not long ago, our team gathered at the Blonde Bar, champagne in hand, sharing burnout stories and fresh ideas. We laughed, we cried, we strategized new guest experiences and mentorship. Each face lit up the room with the same spark I felt when I first believed I could risk everything and win. That shared energy reminds me daily. Leadership isn't a title; it's a light you carry so others can see through their own fog.

Inspiring Others to Leap

If someone asked me now, "What would you tell that terrified woman at the beginning?" I'd say, "Trust yourself enough to start before you're ready." That scary first day on 5th Avenue taught me clarity comes with action. Confidence doesn't precede the first messy steps; it grows because of them.

And I tell that to every stylist, every guest looking into that mirror, every woman standing on her own personal edge. I want them to feel the pull. If I can build this with trembling hands, so can they. House of Blondes isn't just a salon, it's a declaration. Artistry, courage, and joy can coexist. If you step forward, the path will come.

A Horizon Brighter Than Blonde

Ten years in, I look ahead with a heart rooted in the past and eyes hungry for more. Maybe it's training more stylists, or launching a wellness-forward product line, or taking this spirit nationally. But whether I'm refining our color formulas or teaching someone that they're already enough, I'm grateful that one shivering morning turned into a legacy.

So today, when I step into that space bathed in natural light, and hear brushes tickle strands, I feel growth, purpose, and hope. That single moment years ago, me staring in that mirror, willing to fall, flipped the script. Now, as a new mother of a beautiful daughter, Payton, I hope she has my strength and determination to follow her dreams no matter how much they scare her. And I hope others see that they, too, can stand in their mirror, trembling, and whisper, "We're doing this."

About Christina

Christina Payton is a Chicago native who moved to Naples in 2015 with a dream to build an empire. With her big dream and over seventeen years of experience in the hair and beauty industry, she is constantly in pursuit of growth and excellence. Now a well-known and respected salon owner and professional colorist, she has cornered the market in coloring blondes, with The House Of Blondes representing new age artistry in color corrections and hand painting techniques. With her contagious spirit, unwavering drive, and attention to detail, her professional instincts and exceptional artistry skills merge to create transformative results.

Beyond the salon chair, Christina has trained with industry-leading artists to bring her guests the latest trends and techniques. In April 2016, Christina was inducted as the first National Redken Artist in Southwest Florida. In addition to color services, Christina works with many hair extension lines to create fullness and/or length to accommodate all hair goals.

Christina wouldn't have the continued success of her business if it weren't for her incredible team! Between her stylists and assistants, it takes a dream team to accomplish serious hair goals together! Beyond offering a home base for her team, she has designed a branded training program and apprenticeship for all incoming team members. Her dedication to providing continuing education and perfecting the latest techniques shows in the consistency of quality that the staff executes for all guests.

Instagram: TheHouseOfBlondes_
www.thehouseofblondes.com

One Brave Yes at a Time
Jessica Young

I'm Jessica Young, the woman behind SkinCo—a skin-focused med spa in Naples, Fla., where I blend science-backed skincare with soul-deep self-care. As a licensed esthetician, devoted mom, and passionate entrepreneur, my mission is to help people not just look better, but feel deeply seen, safe, and supported in their own skin.

On the surface, SkinCo looks like a place for treatments, lasers, and that lit-from-within glow. But underneath, it's a sanctuary born from survival, built on empathy, and driven by purpose. SkinCo isn't just a business—it's my story, rewritten in real time.

Alongside SkinCo, I also founded Wags to Wishes, a nonprofit dedicated to rescuing animals and supporting the families who love them. Whether it's in my treatment room or in the community, my work is fueled by resilience, rooted in compassion, and unapologetically real.

My love for skincare didn't start early. I wasn't the little girl dreaming of facials or med spas. It came unexpectedly at age twenty-six, when I was still hustling behind the bar, working long nights in the service industry and searching for meaning outside of mixing drinks. After nearly a decade of coasting through shifts, I had a conversation with a coworker that stopped me in my tracks.

"Would you do this all over again?" I asked.

"Absolutely not," she said without hesitation.

That was my wake-up call. Something inside me shifted, and I knew I couldn't keep living on autopilot. Around that time, I had started experimenting with medical-grade skincare—not as a career move, but as a form of self-care. People noticed. Bar regulars asked me what I was using, and before long, I was helping strangers build skincare routines between pouring cocktails.

I loved it. It felt natural, helpful, hopeful—like I was finally tapping into something that lit me up inside. At twenty-seven, I took the leap. I enrolled in esthetics school and poured myself into the science and art of skin. It wasn't just a new career—it was a lifeline. A chance to align my work with a purpose that mattered to me.

Fresh out of school, I knew one thing: if I didn't land a job right away, I'd likely lose my momentum. It was the dead heat of a Naples summer—off-season, when no one was hiring. By a stroke of luck (and friendship), I landed at a local wax center. Not glamorous, but it was a start. For six months, I waxed everything from brows to booty holes. Humbling? Absolutely. But it gave me grit.

Soon after, I landed what I thought was my dream job at a prestigious dermatology office. Clinical, respected, high-volume. I thought I'd retire there. But after two and a half years, reality hit me hard. I felt boxed in by outdated treatments, resistance to innovation, and values that didn't align with mine. I wanted to give clients more—and I knew I couldn't do it there.

So when the chance came, I didn't walk. I ran. And that's how SkinCo was born.

But while I was building a business, I was also surviving something I didn't talk about: an abusive relationship. For three years, I endured a cycle of control, manipulation, and harm. By day, I poured into clients, creating a space of healing and beauty. By night, I questioned my own worth, walking on eggshells. SkinCo became my safe haven, the one place I could shape on my own terms. With every client, I reminded myself of the life I was building—and the woman I was becoming.

Eventually, I left. Not because it was easy, but because I knew I was meant for more—more peace, more joy, more life. And I was right.

Motherhood became my next chapter. When my daughter was born, I felt an immediate, unshakable sense of purpose. She became my greatest teacher and motivation. I didn't just want to build a life for her—I wanted to build an empire where she would always feel safe and supported.

Even on maternity leave, while others expected me to rest, I expanded. I moved SkinCo from a single suite into a brand-new location with multiple treatment rooms, a reception area, and room to grow. I launched The Glow & Go Bar, a mobile extension of SkinCo that brings facials and skincare to private events and pop-ups. And I created NestGuard SWFL, a babyproofing business designed to help parents create safe homes for their little ones—a natural extension of my new season of life.

Motherhood didn't make me smaller. It sharpened my purpose and reminded me that legacy starts at home.

At the same time, I never stopped advocating for those without a voice—the animals. Wags to Wishes became my way of rescuing shelter pets and helping families in crisis keep their beloved animals. Through fundraisers, adoptions, and community events like Puppy Prom, I merged creativity with compassion. Even three months postpartum, I co-hosted the third annual Puppy Prom—because when I commit, I show up.

My story isn't just about survival or success. It's about transformation. From bartending to abuse to entrepreneurship to motherhood, every chapter shaped me into the woman I am today. Healing didn't happen overnight. It came in layers: one client, one tear, one brave yes at a time.

Through therapy, reflection, and the love I pour into my work, I rebuilt myself. I stopped performing and started feeling. I turned wounds into wisdom and wisdom into rebirth.

Today, I live differently. More rooted, more intentional. The glow I help others achieve? I earned it for myself first. And I'm just getting started.

My vision is bold and grounded in the values that built everything I have—authenticity, compassion, and impact. I see SkinCo evolving into a wellness destination. I see NestGuard expanding across Florida. I see Wags to Wishes ensuring no animal or family is left behind.

And most of all, I see my daughter growing up knowing her mom did the work, used her voice, and built a legacy of love, resilience, and purpose. Because when I dream now, I don't just dream for me—I dream for her, and for every woman still finding the strength to begin again.

About Jessica

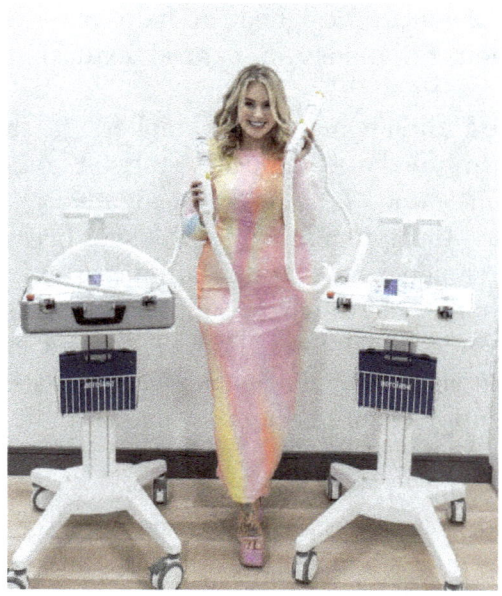

Jessica Young is the founder of SkinCo, a luxury med spa in Naples, Fla., where science-backed skincare meets soulful self-care. A licensed esthetician, devoted mother, and passionate entrepreneur, Jessica has built her career on more than just creating glowing complexions—she's created safe spaces where people feel truly seen and supported in their own skin.

Her path to skincare wasn't traditional. After nearly a decade bartending, Jessica discovered her passion for medical-grade skincare in her mid-twenties, when a casual conversation sparked the realization that she wanted more out of life. What began as a personal self-care ritual evolved into a calling, and she soon enrolled in esthetics school, determined to transform her future.

Jessica's journey hasn't been without hardship. While building her business, she also survived years of abuse, using her work as both an outlet and a lifeline. SkinCo became more than a med spa—it became her sanctuary, a reflection of resilience, and a testament to the healing power of empathy and self-belief.

Motherhood expanded her purpose. Inspired by her daughter, Jessica grew SkinCo into a new multi-room location, launched The Glow & Go Bar for mobile skincare experiences, and created NestGuard SWFL, a babyproofing company dedicated to helping families keep their homes safe.

Beyond skincare, Jessica is also the founder of Wags to Wishes, a nonprofit that supports shelter animals and helps families in crisis keep their pets through funding for food, medical care, and supplies.

Jessica's story is one of reinvention, resilience, and radiant purpose—a glow that shines from the inside out.

Instagram : @skinco_naples

About the Curator, Leigh M. Clark

Four-time best-selling author Leigh M. Clark is known for her inspiring books, including *The Dream is in Your Hands*, *Living Kindly*, and the *Slay the USA* series. Her work as an author has empowered and motivated countless readers by highlighting kindness, resilience, and the strength of community. In addition to her writing career, Leigh has over 20 years of experience as a business strategist, working with Fortune 500 companies to help them grow and succeed.

Leigh's latest project, the Slay the USA series, is a growing national movement that shines a spotlight on extraordinary women across the country who are leaving their mark on their communities and industries. Through this series, Leigh is empowering these women to share their stories of triumph, leadership, and impact, much like she has done in her own life. The series is rapidly expanding, highlighting women in cities from coast to coast, celebrating their contributions and inspiring others to follow their lead.

Leigh's expertise and passion for leadership and empowerment have made her a sought-after speaker, with multiple appearances on the TEDx stage. Her stories of kindness and personal growth have been featured in prominent publications like *HuffPost* and shared through appearances on *The Today Show* and the *Rachael Ray Show*.

As the founder of Kindleigh, a movement focused on giving back through acts of kindness, Leigh has led initiatives that have raised significant funds for charitable causes. Her mission is to create lasting change through kindness and sharing stories of impact, further solidifying her role as a leader in philanthropy.

Leigh resides in Southwest Florida with her son, Carter, and the love of her life. She's here to make an impact and leave her mark by illuminating others.

"Don't let the world change your heart. Let your heart change the world." - Leigh M. Clark

Instagram:@leighmclark @slaytheusa
www.leighmclark.com
www.slaytheusa.com

www.ingramcontent.com/pod-product-compliance
Lightning Source LLC
Chambersburg PA
CBHW071202120626
46546CB00006B/2377